THE LEAVES HAVE LOST
THEIR TREES

The long term effects of a refugee childhood
on ten German-Jewish children who escaped
the Nazi regime

by

Dorothy Marie Darke

William Sessions Limi
York, England

D1206624

© Dorothy Marie Darke

ISBN 1 85072 226 9

Printed from Author's disk
in 11 on 12½ point Times typeface
by Sessions of York
The Ebor Press
York, England

CONTENTS

page

PROLOGUE 1

PART ONE   **INTRODUCING THE WITNESSES**

Ida's Story 7
Renate's Story 8
Frank's Story 11
Kurt's Story 12
Eva's Story 14
Eve's Story 16
Paul's Story 18
Dorothy's Story 20
Luke's Story 23
Ruth's Story 25

PART TWO   **SETTING THE SCENE**

Exodus   The Crucial Decision to Leave   28
In Memoriam 50
Outsiders   Finding an Identity 51

PART THREE   **THE COMMON THREADS**

Reconciliation - Germany 68
Reconciliation - Israel 82
Pacifism 83
Race Relations in Britain 86
Clouded Lives 89
Life Commitments 91
Concluding Reflections 99
Epilogue 104

References 105
Bibliography 107

ILLUSTRATIONS

page

Josef and Bertha Meyer on their Wedding Day viii

Renate and her sister in 1932 9

Frank in 1938 11

Kurt in 1938 13

Eva in 1938 15

Eve in 1939 17

Dorothy with her grandmother in July 1937 22

Luke, Angelica, Ben and Michael with their parents 24

Ruth and her brother: Berlin 1936 25

Eva and her family: a mountaineering weekend 31

Schloss Werther: Kurt's home until 1939 37

Renate's family home in Jocketa, Saxony 39

Frank aged about five, with one of his friends 44

Paul Oestreicher and his father, Dr Paul Oestreicher 46

Eve and her brother at a family swimming party 48

Ruth aged 3 49

Memorial to the victims of the Holocaust in Teresienstadt 50

Renate and her sister 52

Eva playing a violin 55

Ruth on the farm 59

Dorothy 64

Kurt with children of the Nursery Class at Nansen Village 96

Holocaust Memorial in Kibbutz Hazorea 104

ACKNOWLEDGEMENTS

This book is based on a dissertation written in part fulfilment of the requirements for the degree of Master of Advanced Studies at the Department of Peace Studies in the University of Bradford. It was first published in a German translation in May 1998 by Aktion Sühnezeichen Friedensdienste in Berlin, one of four titles published to celebrate their 40th Anniversary. This organisation was founded in 1958 in response to the 'Call for Peace' voiced by the courageous German, Judge Lothar Kressig, who continued to administer justice on his own terms during the Nazi regime and, as a result, was eventually himself sent to a concentration camp. The aim of ASF is to seek reconciliation with nations which suffered under Nazi occupation, or were otherwise affected by the regime, by sending out young German volunteers to work in these countries in social service projects, in peace education and with Jewish communities - especially with those who now care for Jews forced in the 1930s and 1940s to flee their homelands. The British branch of ASF, called Action Reconciliation Services for Peace, is based at the International Centre at Coventry Cathedral. That ASF should have chosen to publish this book is an appropriate ending to the pilgrimage I undertook to discover my past, in memory of my grandparents who were killed in the Holocaust. I had lived most of my life rejecting my roots, believing that I could decide at what precise moment my 'past' began. But to ignore one's heritage is to belittle the whole of life. Without yesterday, today is meaningless, and tomorrow is dangerously threatened. On a plaque at the entrance to Dachau are written these words:

Those who do not remember the past are condemned to repeat it.

That it is Sessions of York – a well established Quaker company, now in its seventh generation of ownership by the family which founded it – who are the publishers of this second edition of my book is a deeply rewarding joy. Not only have I become a Quaker myself, but all those of us who came to Britain as refugees in the 1930s are conscious of the important role the Quakers played in helping Jews to escape from Nazi occupied Europe, and to find sanctuary in Britain where they (and many other groups also) supported and encouraged us in our struggle to create a new life in this our chosen new homeland.

I would like to thank most warmly my nine witnesses for sharing with me so openly and honestly their recollections and life philosophy. Without their sensitive cooperation this book could not have been written. Several were strangers when we first met for this project. I feel privileged now to call them all my friends.

I wish to record my sincere gratitude to Valerie Flessati, who was my tutor for the original dissertation, for her wise guidance, inspiration and unfailing encouragement.

I greatly value and appreciate the contribution made by my husband, Michael, and thank him for his patient understanding of why I set out on this long pilgrimage of discovery.

Finally, I would like to pay special tribute to Gerda Mayer whose poem inspired the title of this book. In it she captures with poignant simplicity the yearning loneliness of a refugee.

I wish to thank the following who have kindly granted permission to quote extracts from the following works:

All the Leaves have lost their Trees. © Gerda Mayer. From *Bernini's Cat (New and Selected Poems)* by Gerda Mayer, Iron Press, 1999. First published in *The Knockabout Show,* Chatto & Windus, 1978

To my Children and *Race* by Karen Gershon. © Macmillan 1989

The Uprooted. © Dorit B. Whiteman

Recollections and Reflections by Bruno Bettelheim. © Thames & Hudson International Ltd. London

...and the Policeman Smiled. © Barry Turner

The Double Cross by Paul Oestreicher. © Darton Longman and Todd London 1986

Aufs Kreuz gelegt by Paul Oestreicher. © Wichern-Verlag Berlin 1993

All attempts at tracing the copyright of the following were unsuccessful

Children of Europe by Dorothy Macardle. Published by Victor Gollancz

Trial and Error: The Autobiography of Chaim Wiezmann. Published by Penguin UK

Josef and Bertha Meyer on their Wedding Day

PROLOGUE

This book is dedicated to my grandparents, Josef and Bertha Meyer. I never knew them because before I was two years old we left Cologne, where I was born, never to live in Germany again. Everyone who knew them spoke of them as gentle, loving people, full of laughter and fun, and immensely generous to their many friends and relatives. In August 1942 they were taken from the train transporting Jews from the infamous Teresienstadt ghetto to Auschwitz, and they were shot by the side of the railway line. This bleak fact I learned from my Israeli aunt only in 1993, when at last I found the courage to ask.

My husband and I have seven greatly loved grandchildren. The relationship between them and us is very close and I realise more and more what I missed in not having had the opportunity to benefit from and cherish that special relationship with my father's parents, and to have been deprived of the unique joy of growing up in the loving, joyful, large extended family of aunts, uncles and cousins from which he came. That whole family was destroyed. Some were murdered in the concentration camps of Nazi-occupied Europe. Others, like us, were forced to flee from all they had known and loved in the land of their birth. Distraught as they were, nevertheless these 'survivors' were safe, and had a second chance to fashion a new life for themselves, as we were able to do, by the good fortune of having found refuge in a friendly country.

It has taken me a lifetime, certainly fifty years, to find the courage to look in depth at the circumstances which brought me and many other refugees to Britain. The interviews I had with nine other people who came here from Germany in the 1930s confirm that for most of us it is only now, as our professional lives are gradually ending, and our children are independent, that we have the inclination to look back, take stock, and try to make sense out of our experiences.

Writing this narrative is the culmination of a long pilgrimage of atonement, reconciliation and self discovery; atonement for the many years during which I turned my back on my origins and ancestry and rejected

1

any connection with my roots; reconciliation as I come to terms with the reality of the events which have shaped our lives; and self discovery as I face, at last without shame, my German and my Jewish heritage. Two events, both of which occurred when I was already over 50 years old, were the catalysts which encouraged me to set out on this pilgrimage. The first was when, as co-ordinator for multicultural education for West Sussex, I organised Racism Awareness Training as part of an In Service Training course for teachers. This training, for which I thought I was so well prepared, turned out to be a deeply disturbing and emotional experience for all of us, but especially perhaps for me! I very quickly realised that I was not the unprejudiced open-minded person I had hoped and thought I was, but held attitudes riddled with ambivalence and shame about my German and my Jewish roots. The second event occurred when I was on a tour of development projects in Orissa, India, organised for Oxfam volunteers. Five of us were scheduled to travel to Bhadrak to visit a women's co-operative craft centre. The four to five hour journey was long, hot and tedious. To pass the time we agreed to tell our life stories. Eve (who is interviewed for this narrative) was the first. She had come to England as a child refugee, fleeing from Nazi persecution of Jews in Czechoslovakia. She expressed many of the feelings I had myself; ambivalence about her origins (as a refugee child she had longed to assimilate completely with her new homeland); an inability to face directly the horror of the Holocaust; a fear of the consequences of finding out too much; a wish not to know. This was the first time that I had ever heard my own feelings so accurately described. I had never considered the possibility that there were hundreds - perhaps thousands - of other people who felt the way I did. That was the beginning of my pilgrimage, although I did not know it at the time.

The narrative is based on interviews with nine people who came to Britain as child refugees in the 1930s. My own experience provides a tenth witness. The interviews were recorded, and I transcribed the tapes verbatim, so that I could quote my witnesses using their own way of expressing their recollections and ideas. Anxious to avoid the danger of imposing my own ideas onto my witnesses, I thought very carefully about how the interviews should be conducted, and decided against any form of questionnaire, or any predetermined schedule of issues to discuss. I tried to make the 'interviews' feel like normal conversations;

therefore many of them were held in my witnesses' own homes. Others were over a relaxed meal, and the fact that a tape recorder was running was quickly forgotten. With very little prompting from me they were soon talking very fluently about their childhood, and about the experiences which led them to their present commitments and value sets. I hope that their unique experiences and the individuality of their different personalities, will therefore shine through the analysis.

Volumes of literature, and innumerable erudite research articles about the Holocaust have been published. It took some years to recover confidence after the war before the truth could be faced and articulated; and then many books were written by and about the survivors of the concentration camps; and a few about adult refugees and their struggle to create a new life for themselves and their families. However, very little was written about the experiences of their children. Those refugees who fled to Britain in the early and mid-1930s faced comparatively few emigration problems. But from 1938 onwards the flight from Germany and occupied territories was fraught with bureaucratic obstacles and dangers. A special effort to rescue the children resulted in the organisation of the Kindertransports which brought 10,000 children to safety in Britain. They left behind them the security of a loving family, a comfortable home, their friends and relatives, to face, alone, an uncertain future in an alien land. Many can scarcely remember saying goodbye to parents they were destined never to see again. It is only comparatively recently that they have begun to tell their stories. Faced by a comparison with the nightmare suffered by those they had left behind they felt they had no story to tell. They were in any case too busily involved in organising their lives, completing their education, finding work, establishing a career, forming relationships and becoming part of the community of their adopted homeland. There was no time or energy left to reflect upon their circumstances. The post-war era was a time when little thought was given to self analysis. One simply accepted one's circumstances and got on with life to the best of one's ability.

At the time of the twenty fifth anniversary of the first Kindertransport, Karen Gershon, who had come to Britain herself as a child refugee through the Zionist Youth Movement, Youth Aliyah, decided to record what information she could. She found that:

> *"Most of the documents of those days have been destroyed, and many of the people who were concerned with our rescue no longer remember the events clearly or...are dead. I decided then to collect what material I could before it was too late."*   *(1)*

The result was a book, *We Came As Children*, published in 1966, which is a collective autobiography, the edited recollections of 234 former child refugees who responded to a request for information published in all the major newspapers; Kurt - one of my witnesses - is also quoted in Karen Gershon's book. In 1989 this book was republished to back up a BBC programme marking the fiftieth anniversary of the first Kindertransport. By now it was recognised that there was indeed a story to tell. Several more books based on interviews were published; those to which I have referred are listed in the bibliography. Two are particularly important. One by Barry Turner, called *...And The Policeman Smiled*, is based on an unspecified number of interviews and previously unpublished records and letters. This has been an invaluable source of background information. The other is by Dorit Bader Whiteman, a clinical psychologist and herself a child refugee who, with her family, found sanctuary in New York. *The Uprooted - A Hitler Legacy* is based on the testimony of 190 refugees. Their stories are told largely in their own words, but Dr Whiteman provides important insights into the long term effects of their wartime experience as they were:

> *"...struggling to settle in a new land, unable to speak the language, without appropriate skills or education, without money or contacts and filled with uncertainty over the fate of family and friends."*   *(2)*

Dr Whiteman's book, published in 1993, was at that time the most widely researched book of its kind, focussing on the events of the time and the traumatic readjustments that were necessary as the refugees began to rebuild their shattered lives. These are moving accounts of a short dramatic period in the lives of these 'uprooted' people and its immediate after-effects. Dr Whiteman also includes a very valuable section at the end of her book analysing the long term psychological effects of these experiences. Our narrative differs in emphasis from the other books to which I have referred. We ten are now nearing the end of our professional working lives, or have already retired. The purpose of this book is to look back, and to set our childhood experience into the context of a whole working life time. Some of us have had little time or wish to give much thought to this experience. But now we have reached a stage when it is natural to look back, and the long term impact on our attitudes and perceptions of the world around us is becoming clearer. The more I talked to the members of my 'witness group' the more I became conscious of the common threads of our experience, and that as a result we have a similar outlook upon the world around us. I have tried to describe some of the attitudes we hold in common. Most of us were able to adapt to our new life quite easily, especially those of us who left Germany with our parents. But for some, the comparatively short time of being uprooted and of growing up in an alien environment was so powerful that it set the agenda for life.

The evidence of ten witnesses encompasses too narrow a spectrum to claim that any far-reaching conclusions can be drawn. Our parents were, in any case, not a cross-representative section of the German Jewish society of their day, and our experience is that of children who came from well established middle class professional or business families. Our parents had felt themselves to be very firmly rooted in the mainstream of German cultural and social life. My witnesses have another characteristic in common. They have all, in their different and individual ways, made a success of their lives, and have therefore been able to make a valuable contribution to the life of their adopted homeland. They have shown courage, determination, perseverance and commitment. It is just these qualities which have enabled Jewish culture and religion to survive centuries of persecution. Their families had thought of themselves as totally assimilated into the social fabric of the land of their birth. We ten now feel ourselves to be totally British, and are proud to be so! The wheel has turned full circle.

It has been a privilege to talk to my nine witnesses, and I would like to record my sincere thanks to them for their generosity in giving me so much of their time, for answering my questions so openly and honestly, and for sharing with me their memories and their feelings. What I hope to show from their evidence is that, tragic and terrible as these events were at the time, for these nine people at least, the consequences have not been totally negative. Exposed to prejudice and alienation at an early age, some of them witnessing scenes of barbaric cruelty against those they loved for no reason other than their parentage, they have developed a heightened awareness of injustice, prejudice and discrimination in the world around them. For three in particular, Kurt, Paul and Ruth, this awareness has led directly to a life of service for others in similarly difficult or distressing circumstances. For others in our group, the link between their experience and their career is not so obvious, but their commitment to the causes of freedom and peace shines clearly in their testimony.

PART ONE

INTRODUCING THE WITNESSES

IDA'S STORY   born in 1922

Ida was born in Dortmund where her father was a legal adviser to a bank. Her mother came from the city of Minden. When, in 1924, Ida's grandfather had his first heart attack, her family moved to Minden so that her father could help to run his father-in-law's bank, the Bankhaus Steinfeldt.

Ida's childhood in Minden was very happy. She enjoyed school, and had many friends. Her particular interest was in science and from an early age she hoped to become a doctor. She also attended Jewish religious class every Sunday, although her father was a freethinker and encouraged Ida to be liberal in her attitudes and to respect the religious beliefs of others. The family social life was not exclusively within the Jewish community but encompassed a wide circle of friends, so it came as a profound shock for Ida's parents to find that their Jewish heredity set them apart. As anti-Semitic Nazi propaganda began to have its effect many non-Jewish friends began to desert them, and in 1937, at the age of only 15, Ida was forced to leave school, shattering her hopes of studying medicine at university.

Ida's parents now became involved in helping other Jewish families to emigrate. Her father organised, as far as he could, their legal affairs; her mother taught English and Spanish to prepare her students for life in a new homeland. Realising that they had no future in Germany either, they also began the search for a safe haven for themselves. A family friend, who had already emigrated to Britain, was eventually successful in arranging a traineeship for Ida which entitled her to enter Britain. She left Germany in the summer of 1939. She was never to see her parents or her many close relatives again.

In Birmingham Ida lived in a refugee hostel and worked as a trainee at a children's clothing factory. It was tedious work, alleviated only by the satisfaction she got from studying chemistry at weekend adult education classes at Birmingham Technical College. Six months after the outbreak of war the factory was destroyed in an air raid. Ida was fortunate to be offered an office job quite quickly and was soon promoted to become personal assistant to the manager. Meanwhile her enthusiasm for chemistry continued and she was rewarded eventually by the offer of a job as assistant in a laboratory testing metal for the manufacture of ammunition.

At about this time she moved to another hostel for German speaking Jewish refugees in Edgbaston. Because she was studying she was given a small bedroom to share with just one other girl, so that she could work undisturbed. Unfortunately this excellent arrangement did not last long. Two students in their final year of study at the University of Birmingham were considered to have a greater priority for quiet study facilities, and Ida and her friend were moved to a dormitory with several other girls. One of those students was Franzl Wallach - a young engineer. It was not long before Ida and Franzl (Frank) were friends, and when he graduated in June 1946 they were married.

Ida passed her matriculation which enabled her to study biology at university. She became a teacher and her professional experience spans a wide range of schools including a particularly fulfilling period at a special school for partially-hearing partially-sighted children. Her last job was at the Royal School in Bath where she became careers mistress and sixth form tutor in addition to teaching science. Although she was not able to achieve her early ambition of becoming a doctor, Ida did find in teaching an outlet for her wish to be of service to the community. A particularly happy postscript is that all three of Frank and Ida's children are now practising medicine.

RENATE'S STORY   born in 1923

Renate was born in Plauen. Her father, who was Jewish, was a junior partner in his family's lace-making factory. It was an international business exporting lace all over the world, and he had special responsibility for export sales to England. Her mother had also worked as an apprentice in this firm, and married her father after his return from service with the army during the First World War. At this time he became baptised as a Christian, in solidarity with his wife, who came from a Lutheran background.

Renate and her younger sister in 1932: a skiing holiday in Berwang (on a South facing slope!)

Because of his responsibility for exports to England, Renate's father spent much of his working time in Britain and had many business colleagues and friends here. He was very well informed politically, so when Hitler came to power in 1933 he made arrangements to move his family to England. However it was not until 1935 that Renate's family left Germany to settle in London. By now the firm was managed by non-Jewish members of the family, who enabled Renate's father to remain on the payroll as manager of exports to England, although he was forced to resign from his position as a junior partner to comply with Nazi regulations. When war was declared this arrangement came to an abrupt end. Renate's father tried to set up some small business enterprise of his own, at first without success, so life was a tough struggle. He was eventually successful in launching a small firm making high-quality blouses.

Because of these financial constraints Renate had to leave school when she was 16. She had already decided to work with young children, and to gain experience became an assistant at a kindergarten near her home. This was to have been for just one year, but the family budget could not stretch to cover the cost of college fees, and in any case her job as an assistant teacher was classified as 'war work'. It was not until these 'war work' regulations were relaxed in 1944, nearly five years later, that she was able to start her professional training at the Froebel Institute in Roehampton.

Renate enjoyed college and gained a distinction in her final exams. Her first post was at a private junior school where she taught for five years. To broaden her experience she then moved to a state school in Highgate where the children came from a range of different social and racial backgrounds. She taught there for three years. After a year of further study at London University, Renate was appointed as Senior Mistress at a school in Crouch End where again the children came from a variety of backgrounds, and often from socially deprived homes. The nine years she worked here were stimulating and happy, but colleagues were urging her to move on, perhaps to become involved in teacher training. In spite of her reluctance to lose direct classroom contact with the children, she was eventually persuaded to apply for a job with the National Inspectorate of Schools, and was appointed as an HMI in 1965. It was a challenging job that involved inspection visits to schools, and also In Service Training for teachers, lecturers and local authority advisers from all over England. Renate's commitment to the opportunities and demands of this responsibility left little time for any outside activities. The almost twenty years she gave to service with the National Inspectorate were a rewarding culmination to a lifetime of dedication to education.

FRANK'S STORY   born in 1924

Frank's father, Max, was the fourth of ten children born between 1871 and 1888 to Julia and Heinemann Wallach of Bielefeld. Two of his brothers, Julius and Moritz, studied folk art, first in their native Westphalia, later broadening their knowledge and expertise to include folk art tradition throughout Germany and Austria. On this knowledge was based the craft work of the Volkskunsthaus Wallach, which became

Frank in 1938: a year before he left Germany on the Kindertransport

an internationally known centre of German and Austrian folk art in Munich. Max became an engineer and travelled widely before re-settling in Germany in the 1920s to take charge of the handwork printing plant of the Volkskunsthaus Wallach in the Munich suburb of Dachau. Here he met and married Melanie. Frank was their only child.

Frank has happy memories of homelife and schooldays. At the Volksschule in Dachau his class teachers were staunch Catholics and coura-geously anti-Nazi. In 1934 he transferred to the Gisela Oberrealschule in Munich. Here also the headmaster gave a determined lead in creating an atmosphere in which the Jewish pupils could prosper on equal terms with the majority of children who came from Catholic families.

It was not until Kristallnacht that Frank experienced his first taste of per-secution and brutality against the Jews. Then life changed abruptly. He and his parents were forced to leave their home that night, never to return. They fled to the mountains south of Munich, where they could stay in comparative safety with friends who owned a farm, until the immediate danger was over. From that time on until the end of July 1939, when he was finally able to leave Germany with the Kindertransport, Frank felt constantly under threat.

He lived during these desperate months with his mother's sister in Paderborn, no longer able to go to school, but studying English and Spanish to prepare for life in another country. A family friend who had already emigrated to England, offered to be guarantor to enable him to come to Britain. He left Germany in August 1939. Sadly, in spite of frantic efforts to find a place of refuge, Frank's parents were unable to escape in time.

In England Frank continued his education under the auspices of the Church of England Committee for Refugees, who sent him first to Monkton Combe School in Bath, and then to Dean Close School in Cheltenham, where he passed his Higher School Certificate in 1941. A scholarship enabled him to study engineering at the University of Birmingham. In his final year he found accommodation in a hostel for German-speaking Jewish refugees, where he met Ida, who became his wife.

Frank stayed at Birmingham to do research, for which he gained a PhD and an appointment on the teaching staff. He moved to Queen's University Belfast in 1959, returning to England in 1966 to take up an appointment as Professor of Mechanical Engineering at the University of Bath. During more than twenty-five years in charge of this department he was conspicuous in his success in attracting industrial sponsorship and funding for research.

KURT'S STORY   born in 1924

Kurt's parents lived in the village of Werther, near Bielefeld, where his grandfather had bought the old mansion house, Schloss Werther, both as a home and as a site for a cigar factory. Kurt grew up here, with an older brother and younger twin sisters, in what he remembers as an idyllic childhood environment. His mother came from Bremen, where his father had been apprenticed for some time to learn about the tobacco trade.

Kurt was shy and sensitive as a boy. He attended the Volksschule in Werther and was well aware of the pro-Nazi attitude of the headmaster, who was wont to come to school wearing his SA uniform. Fortunately his form master was not a Nazi supporter. After three years at the village Church School he was sent to Frankfurt to board with a teacher so that he could attend the Jewish School there. It was not a happy experience. He felt lonely and isolated in the impersonal disciplinarian ethos of this very large school.

Kurt in 1938

By the mid 1930s severe restrictions had been imposed on the management of the cigar factory and eventually Kurt's father was forced to 'sell' ('transfer' would be a more accurate term) his business to an 'Aryan' competitor in a nearby town. Clearly there was no future for the family in Germany and the search for a new homeland began. The terrible events of Kristallnacht, when Kurt's father was arrested and sent to Buchenwald concentration camp for five weeks, added a desperate urgency to the search for a way out. Kurt and his brother and sisters were able to leave Germany on Kindertransports during the summer of 1939. Kurt's mother, who had organised the family's 'Auswanderung' on her own because his father was confined to hospital after his release from Buchenwald, was eventually successful in obtaining entry to Britain for both herself and her husband. They left Germany only just in time at the end of August.

In England Kurt lodged with Liesel Fleck and her mother, themselves of German origin, who were devoted guardians. He was fortunate to be befriended by Mrs Aitken, who had given a house to the Fleck family for use as an Old Age Home for Jewish refugees. She paid the fees for his first summer term at Christ's College in Blackheath. When war was declared the school was evacuated to Treverven in Cornwall. The Headmaster, Alex Crombie, generously covered the cost of tuition himself so that Kurt was able to complete his education at the school as a boarder. Kurt would like to have studied engineering, but by the time he left school in 1942 he was too old for an apprenticeship, and university fees were out of the question. He found employment first at a radio repair shop, and later at a radio factory in Tottenham. His father meanwhile had been working as a gardener and also on a farm near Banbury, gradually regaining his health. Kurt's brother had been sent to Canada in 1940 instead of being interned in Britain. In 1944 the rest of the family were at last able to set up home and live together for the first time since they were parted in 1939.

After the war the cigar factory was returned to Kurt's father under the German government restitution programme, but he was in no condition to undertake its management. It fell to Kurt to return, unwillingly, to Werther in 1950 to manage the factory until he was able to arrange a sale to the former factory manager, who had throughout done what he could to help the family through their ordeal. In 1954 Kurt was able to return to London where he set up his own cigar import business.

Kurt's wife, Charlotte, was also a Jewish refugee from Germany, whose family had found sanctuary in New York. The difficulties Kurt and Charlotte had faced themselves in growing up as aliens, in a friendly but nonetheless unfamiliar environment, encouraged them to help foreign students. They decided to set up a housing association in North London for foreign postgraduate students, known as Nansen Village. Concern for the administration and continued viability of Nansen Village, as well as for the personal welfare of all the residents, has been a full-time commitment to which Kurt and Charlotte have dedicated themselves for over 30 years.

EVA'S STORY   born in 1928

Eva was born in Wurzburg, but grew up with her older brother, Rolf, in Munich. Her father had an influential post as a lawyer in the civil service.

He came from a well established Jewish family from Wurzburg, where his mother was known as an accomplished pianist. He had wanted to study music, but this was not considered to be an acceptable profession, so he was persuaded to study law instead.

Eva in 1938

Eva's mother was the daughter of Professor Julius Schmidt of Stuttgart University, whose text book on chemistry was the standard reference used by the universities of that time. His wife, Isabella, was a pianist, well known on the concert platforms of Southern Germany, and a formidable character in her own right.

Eva's family were well integrated into the life of Munich society. Most of their friends were musicians; many were Jewish, but by no means all, and her parents identified strongly with German cultural and social life. Until the mid-1930s life was very comfortable, and although Eva's father was dismissed from the civil service, as were all Jews in 1934, he received a generous pension and felt reasonably confident about the future. She remembers being very happy at school although in fact she went to six schools before the age of eleven, being rejected by one after another because of her Jewish parentage.

On Kristallnacht everything changed. Eva's father was arrested in the early hours of the morning and sent to Dachau concentration camp, and the family were also threatened. During the five weeks he was imprisoned, Eva's mother began the desperate search for some place of refuge to which they could escape. A family friend, who had already emigrated to South Wales, was able to arrange sponsorship. It took two months of frantic effort to satisfy the obstructively unpredictable bureaucracy necessary for emigration, but the formalities were eventually completed and the family were able to leave Germany in July 1939. They settled in Penarth, but the regulations for their entry to Britain did not allow them to look for work, so life was a constant struggle to make ends meet.

Eva's father found solace through his music, organising a string quartet soon after his arrival in which he played first violin. It was through this music making that Eva met her future husband, for the sister of the second violin was to become Eva's mother-in-law! When France fell in 1940, 'enemy aliens' were no longer allowed to live within ten miles of the coast, so the family moved to Gilwern, near Abergavenny, and Eva's father was interned for a few weeks. By the time he was released the restrictions on work permits for refugees had been relaxed, so once again Eva's father turned to music, building up a successful career as a teacher of violin, viola and piano, travelling the valleys of South Wales to teach his pupils in their own homes. Her mother also contributed to the family income by teaching German to the troops stationed nearby. Such was his reputation that Eva's father was eventually appointed as Head of Strings at Monmouth Public School and Professor of Violin at the Cardiff School of Music and Drama. Sadly, just before he could take up these appointments he died of cancer at the age of only 59. Eva's mother also died of cancer 7 years later.

Eva meanwhile had begun her own career in music. Rowsby Woof, one of the great violin teachers of his day, had heard her play and was so impressed that he offered to teach her free of charge. At the early age of fourteen Eva won a scholarship to study full time at the Royal Academy of Music in London. When she graduated she became a founder member of the London Mozart Players to whom she gave a lifetime of talent and commitment. She added teaching to her very busy concert schedule and drew great satisfaction and pleasure from this opportunity to pass on her own enjoyment of music to a younger generation.

EVE'S STORY   born in 1931

Eve was born in Prague where her father practised as a lawyer. She had a brother, Thomas, three years older than herself. They lived very comfortably in a first floor flat above the office where her father worked, and she remembers the companionship of a large extended family of aunts, uncles, and cousins, with frequent family visits. Her parents were both Jewish, but did not practise their religion at home nor regularly attend synagogue. Like many professional people in the Prague of that time they had been brought up to speak German, and socially that was the accepted language of their generation, but Eve's generation of children usually spoke Czech. At six years old, she started school at the Lycée, where only French was spoken, and she soon became fluent in this second language.

Eve in 1939:
at about the time of her emigration

The German invasion of Czechoslovakia in March 1939 brought about an abrupt change. Fear and tension dominated family life. Eve was able to continue her schooling at the Lycée, but there was much talk about where the Jewish pupils at the school might go to seek refuge from the Nazi threat.

The Kindertransport from Czechoslovakia was quickly organised. Eve's parents were able to arrange for her to be fostered in England, and she left Prague on 31 July. No plans had been made by her parents for their own escape. She never saw her brother or her parents again.

Eve's new home was in the Midlands. Her foster mother, Minnie, was a primary school teacher, whose long experience with young children enabled her to provide all the understanding and security that a confused and emotionally exhausted eight year old needed. It was not long before a stable and loving relationship developed between Eve and her new 'Mum'. She enjoyed school, especially French which she later studied at the University of Hull, and she became a teacher.

Eve's first job was at a school in Aylesbury. But when Minnie became ill she returned to her home town to look after her, and continued her teaching career there. The third school she taught at became a comprehensive school in 1973, at which time she was appointed deputy head, a post she occupied until her retirement in 1985. Being deputy head involved a lot of administration, which cut down the amount of teaching she could do, a cause of some frustration because it was the contact with the children which she enjoyed most in her profession. However, Eve found that even administration had its own interest and rewards, and she feels that her life in education enabled her to make a worthwhile contribution to the community which had given her a new home. After her retirement she became involved in voluntary work on behalf of Oxfam. She also used her experience as a language teacher to teach English to a young Pakistani woman. These voluntary commitments were a direct response, Eve feels, to her own experience of life as a child refugee.

PAUL'S STORY   born in 1931

Paul's father came from a Jewish family, so firmly rooted in mainstream German society that they were hardly aware of their Judaism. He was only eighteen when the First World War broke out and he spent the whole war period in the trenches of Northern France. This war experience was the catalyst which prompted his conversion to Christianity. After the war he studied medicine and as a young doctor he was baptised. He set up a practice as a paediatrician in Thüringen and it was here that he met his wife. She was a singer with the opera in Meiningen and came from a typical German country family.

Paul's parents enjoyed a very pleasant social life in Thüringen, involved in church and cultural activities in the community. The contribution made by Paul's father as a paediatrician was greatly respected, and his practice flourished until the mid-1930s. By 1936, as people became increasingly afraid of official hostility towards anyone who continued to consult Jewish professionals, his patients deserted him. The practice dwindled, and by 1937 he was no longer allowed to practise as a doctor. Paul, who was their only child, started school at the Volksschule, but after only one term, in the Spring of 1938, so ominous was the threat of arrest that Paul's parents fled to Berlin. Here Paul was hidden in the basement flat of a friend, while his parents avoided detection by lodging in a different house each night. They devoted all their time and energy to the search for a safe haven to which they could emigrate. Eventually a medical colleague of Paul's father, who had already emigrated to New Zealand, offered to be a guarantor. All obstacles were eventually overcome and the family set sail for their new homeland in the Spring of 1939.

There were many difficulties to face in trying to build a new life in New Zealand. Refugees were not made very welcome, and because of high levels of unemployment there was a climate of protectionism. The New Zealand Medical Association insisted that all refugee doctors, whatever their qualifications and experience must complete a three-year full-time clinical course before being allowed to practise. While Paul's father was concentrating on this medical course, his mother was earning the family income by running their very large rented house as a student hostel, and by singing in concerts.

Paul's parents spoke German at home, so Paul grew up to be bilingual. He was a high achiever at school and went on to study politics at university. Here his interest in religion deepened and he planned to study at an English theological college. He took advantage, first, of a postgraduate fellowship for study in Germany being offered by the German Embassy, but stayed for only one year before coming to England to continue his studies at Lincoln Theological College. Soon after his arrival in Lincoln he met a newly qualified German physiotherapist, on a year of work experience at Lincoln General Hospital. Lore, who had been born within walking distance of Paul's birthplace, became his wife.

Paul's life has been a powerful mixture of politics and religion. For four years, from 1961, he was at the BBC on the editorial staff of Church and Society, so he had the opportunity to make the connection clear through his broadcasts. In 1964 he was appointed Associate Secretary to the Department of International Affairs of the British Council of

Churches. At first this was a full-time commitment, but in 1968 he became vicar of Blackheath as well. He also became a Quaker, which caused some controversy at the time, though dual Church membership is not unusual nowadays. In 1981 he returned full-time to the British Council of Churches as Head of the Foreign Department until 1986 when he was appointed Director of International Ministry at Coventry Cathedral. In addition to these commitments Paul was, from 1956 until the fall of the communist regimes in Eastern Europe, responsible for the support given by the British Council of Churches to the Churches of Eastern Europe. He also became Vice President of CND and Chairman of the British section of Amnesty International. To all these commitments Paul has been able to bring an awareness enlightened by his own experiences.

DOROTHY'S STORY   born in 1932

My father was born and brought up in Bielefeld. He was the eldest of three children and part of a very large and close-knit extended family. Julia Wallach, the mother of Moritz and Julius who founded the Volkskunsthaus Wallach, and of Max (Frank's father), was my father's great aunt. She lived in Bielefeld and her home was the centre of a very active family social life, and there were many cousins and second cousins who were my father's friends. This strong feeling of family kinship is typically Jewish, but they were not, as far as I know, deeply involved with Judaism as a religion.

My mother came from a typical Württemberg country family. One of her grandfathers owned a farm which has been in the family since the fifteenth century. Her other grandfather was a miller. There was a feeling of being firmly rooted in country life, although my mother actually grew up in Stuttgart, where her father was Director of Postal Services for Württemberg. When my mother told her family of her decision to marry my father - a Jew - there was fierce opposition. Neither her parents nor any of her relatives came to her wedding. She, on the other hand,

20

had been warmly and generously welcomed by my father's family and friends. After their marriage the *fait accompli* was accepted by my mother's family. As they began to know my father better, the ice melted, and my grandmother became devoted to him.

I was born in Cologne, where my father was a partner in his uncle's chamois leather factory, with special responsibility for exports. Sales to Britain were particularly successful, so he came often and had many good friends in the leather trade here. His experience of travelling and talking to many people from different backgrounds gave him an unusually realistic understanding of political developments in Germany. As early as 1933 he made arrangements for our family to emigrate to Britain. Unfortunately, just as the legal formalities for this move were completed, he became ill and tuberculosis of the bone was diagnosed. In those days the only cure was rest and recuperation in the fresh air of the mountains. So early in 1934 we moved instead to Switzerland, where in the spartan regime of a TB clinic, which kept its patients in bed on open balconies, winter and summer, he gradually recovered.

Meanwhile conditions for Jewish businesses in Germany were becoming increasingly difficult. My father had continued to receive a salary during his illness, but in 1936 the business, like other Jewish companies, was transferred to 'Aryan' management. He was forced to resign. Although he had by no means fully recovered he could no longer afford the 'luxury' of being an invalid. He left the clinic, threw away his crutches, and came to England to set up, with the help of his many English friends, his own chamois leather company.

My father did not return to Germany until after the war. For my mother it was quite safe to travel there, so in order to give them both time to concentrate on establishing their new life in England, she left me with her family in Tübingen. I was at first very distressed to be parted from my parents and older sister, but eventually was so happy with my grandmother that when my mother came to fetch me, about a year later in August 1937, I did not want to be parted from my grandmother and return to England with her.

Dorothy with her grandmother in July 1937

I have no recollection of finding my new life in London strange, nor of having any difficulty settling into primary school only four weeks after my arrival. In 1940, as the air raids on London intensified, and France fell, an invasion seemed likely, so my sister and I were sent to boarding school.

The Abbey in Malvern Wells was a typical middle-ranking public school. I was miserably home sick for the first two years, but eventually was very happy in the spartan, sporty, not super-academic ethos. I was there for ten years, and became in thought, word and deed indistinguishable from anyone else educated under the public school system of that time. The experience stood me in good stead for I felt very much at ease with the English way of life, although I had deep-rooted hang-ups about my German origin.

I studied geography at Cambridge, married early and was extremely happy with my very English, ex-RAF architect husband, finding complete fulfilment as wife, mother of four and part-time teacher at our local grammar school. When my husband retired we moved to West Sussex. I became an education volunteer for Oxfam, which led eventually to a part-time post as Multicultural Education Co-ordinator for West Sussex Education Authority, focussing mainly on In Service Training for teachers. I was able to bring to this work my own awareness of how it feels to be 'different' and of how most children from ethnic or national minority background long to be accepted as equal and as 'ordinary'. I know also how easily children's self esteem can be damaged unless their cultural identity is affirmed and seen to be valued and respected.

LUKE'S STORY   born in 1935

Luke's father came from a Jewish family living in Erfurt, and at the early age of thirteen, when his own father died, he took responsibility for the welfare of his mother and sister. As soon as he was able to do so he became the family provider, building up a very successful legal practice in Berlin. His success came early and even before he was fully quali-fied he worked for several very eminent clients. Luke's mother was born in Holland and came from a Protestant family. They had four chil-dren; Michael, born in 1933, Luke in 1935 and Angelica in 1937 were all born while the family lived in Berlin. Ben was born after the family had come to live in England.

Although Luke's father had every reason to think of himself as a good German citizen, he was aware already by the early 1930s that life under Nazi rule would be intolerable. Such was his unease with political develop-ments in Germany that he gave up his legal practice in 1934 and came to Britain for six months to find out if he could establish a new life here for his family. Realising that he might make a success out of setting up a printing company, he returned to Germany to buy printing presses, and machinery for photogravure. Arrangements for emigration were still com-paratively straightforward when the family came to Britain in 1937. In partnership with a Jewish friend from Berlin, an expert printer who left Germany at the same time, Luke's father set up the new company in Slough.

Luke went to the local primary school and then to St Paul's in London where there were many other boys of Jewish parentage. He enjoyed

Luke, Angelica, Ben and Michael with their parents

school and integrated well into all aspects of school life. Because he was a good 'all rounder' a decision about a career was difficult, but he has never regretted his choice of medicine. He studied first at a medical school in London, then at the University of Cambridge, coming back to London to St Mary's Hospital for experience as a junior doctor. After additional training in psychiatry and in paediatrics he joined the newly-formed Department of General Practice at the University of Edinburgh Medical School, the first department in the UK to offer undergraduates as well as postgraduates experience and training in this important area of medicine.

After five years in Edinburgh, Luke returned to London to join a colleague who was setting up a similar department at St Thomas' Hospital, where he has now been for nearly thirty years. His time is divided between teaching, and research, and being 'an ordinary GP' in a practice near St Thomas'. For the patients this practice is a normal medical centre offering a full range of services for health care, but it also acts as a teaching base for students. Luke is sometimes said to be a workaholic. He answers that he is not obsessive about work, but just enjoys every aspect of his career.

RUTH'S STORY   born in 1935

Ruth's family lived in Berlin. Her father was a successful lawyer, who had been brought up in the comfortable security of a typical middle class Jewish home. His mother ran an advertising agency in which Ruth's mother worked as a secretary. It was here that she met her future husband, but she was not Jewish, and this created difficulties from the beginning. Political opinion had already turned against 'mixed marriages' so there

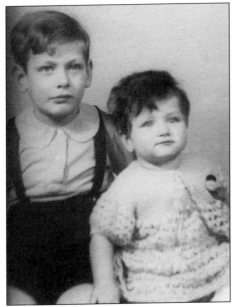

was considerable opposition to the continued relationship from both families. The young couple were married nevertheless and a few years later Ruth's father converted to Christianity. She and her older brother, Martin, were also baptised at this time.

By 1937 life had become very tense and threatening. Ruth's father was planning to emigrate, but his mother was ill and did not want to leave Germany, and she made it difficult for her son to take his family to safety. However, Ruth's parents made arrangements for the children to find refuge in Britain and in the summer of 1939, when Ruth

Ruth and her brother:
Berlin 1936

was only four years old, and Martin was seven, they were brought to a foster home in Kent.

Ruth's early years in Britain were very unsettled. In the first five years she and Martin lived at two different foster homes, a boarding school and a very disorganised hostel. It was not until 1944, when they were sent to their third foster home, that they found the security of a disciplined but affectionate family environment. It proved to be an ideal home, on a farm, with other children for companionship.

Throughout these years there had been a sporadic correspondence through the Red Cross with Ruth's father, who had managed to emigrate to Shanghai after his mother's death in May 1939. He returned to Germany after the war to rebuild his career as a lawyer in Mainz. All contact with Ruth's mother was lost however until she was traced by the Red Cross in 1947. It was not until 1949 that she eventually made contact with Ruth and Martin. By now the separation had been so long that it proved very difficult to rebuild any feeling of kinship. Much against her will, Ruth was forced to leave Martin and her foster parents and return to Germany to live with her parents. It was a disastrous experiment, and after six miserable months she was allowed to return to the family and the life to which she was by now so firmly attached.

Ruth decided to make farming her career. She studied dairy technology at the University of Reading. Here she met Bernard, a student of Education Psychology. The fact that he was of Jewish parentage was an added attraction. Like Ruth, Bernard had not had any formal Jewish religious education, so after their marriage they discovered Judaism together.

While Bernard was completing his training Ruth took a job in research and development at a biscuit factory. It was boring and unrewarding work. Bernard's involvement in education encouraged her to turn to teaching as a career. She took time off while her three children were young, returning to teach at a large comprehensive school when the youngest started school full-time. Her main subject was biology, but it was not long before she became a Head of House, and the pastoral care of her pupils became her greatest concern. To fulfil this responsibility more effectively she took training as a counsellor, and then as a marriage guidance counsellor, which led to an interest in psychotherapy. After several years of further study and training Ruth qualified as a psychotherapist, and it is in this profession that she has found complete fulfilment. She brings to this work an understanding of the effects of a disturbed and troubled childhood. Through the LINK Psychotherapy Centre and through Shelvata, which are Jewish advice and help centres, Ruth is offering specialist help to Holocaust survivors, and refugees, and to their children. She is able to bring to this work a unique insight into their suffering because of all she had experienced herself as a result of racial persecution.

PART TWO   SETTING THE SCENE

TO MY CHILDREN   by Karen Gershon

Others may pity me but you shall not be ashamed
how can I scorn the life which is all I have
I will not belittle the little that I have saved
by denying my childhood memories my love

How can I wish to undo the past which I am
though I beggared myself I would not become another
'the appalling Jewish experience' is my own
'the unknown victims' are my father and mother

Be proud of the beginnings you have in me
be proud of how far I have wandered with this burden
I would value you less if I were not a refugee
your presence changes my wilderness to a garden

Reprinted by kind permission of Macmillan Press from
We Came As Children edited by Karen Gershon
Papermac 1989   (3)

EXODUS   THE CRUCIAL DECISION TO LEAVE

For hundreds of years the Jews of most Western European nations, of Germany and Austria, Britain and France amongst others, had been deprived of the full rights of citizenship. They were barred from many professions and occupations and from an active role in politics; for example, from the judiciary, from the civil service, from most universities and from military service. During the nineteenth century restrictions were gradually relaxed so that before the turn of the century they were able to participate fully in the life of their nation. Encouraged by the new opportunities, the Jewish contribution to the cultural and economic life of Europe was impressive, and they assimilated deeply into the social structures of their homelands. They were now entitled for the first time to enlist in the forces and felt that they had proved their loyalty by their service during the First World War, and had earned their place as respected citizens with the same political and legal rights as their compatriots. By the 1920s they identified themselves as German or Austrian, British or French who happened to be Jewish rather than as Jews who lived in Germany or Austria, Britain or France.

This degree of national identity was felt by the parents of all my witnesses. Six had fathers who were old enough to have fought in the First World War. All had distinguished themselves and five were awarded the highest medal for valour, the Iron Cross - First Class. Ida's comments are typical of our group:

> "As a family we had always been conscious of the fact
> that we were Jews, but we considered ourselves fore-
> most as Germans. My father had fought as a volunteer
> in World War 1, had been wounded in the Battle of Verdun
> and was awarded the Iron Cross. My mother had been
> a sister in the Red Cross and she too was awarded a
> medal."

Paul, also, describes his father as a very patriotic German:

> "My father came of a professional, very nationalistic
> German Jewish family, who were hardly aware of their

28

*Judaism.   He was 18 when World War 1 started - just
the age when he could volunteer.   He went through the
whole war in France.   The only one in his artillery
battery to survive, he was awarded the Iron Cross - First
Class."*

This feeling of being accepted as equal members of the national community, and no different from other citizens, was reflected in the number
of mixed marriages which were common in the Jewish community at
that time. Of our small group of ten, five of us - Renate, Paul, Luke,
Ruth and I - had non-Jewish mothers.   However, 'marrying out' was
less common for Jewish women than for Jewish men, probably because
the traditional doctrine that Jewishness is passed on through the mother
to her child was still a strong influence within Jewish families. Daughters
were considerably more likely than were sons to respond to family pressure and conform to this doctrine by marrying a Jewish partner.

The degree of assimilation was further reinforced by the fact that some
Jews converted to Christianity; some, like Paul's father, out of deep conviction; others perhaps as much for social as for spiritual reasons. Barry
Turner writes that even before the First World War, German Jews felt
they were:

> *"...rooted in a strong sense of national identity with
> national aspirations.   There was no way in which they
> could be judged as essentially different from other
> Germans.   After all, they shared a history going back a
> thousand years.   German industry, law, medicine,
> science, literature and art drew heavily on Jewish
> talent."*   (4)

But defeat in the war shattered the pride of the German nation. During
the 1920s the German economy collapsed. Unemployment led to widespread poverty and dissatisfaction. The hunt for scapegoats was perhaps
predictable. Nevertheless, when Hitler's book *Mein Kampf* was first
published in 1924, very few people inside or outside Germany took it,
or its author, seriously. In it his agenda of despoliation, persecution and
ultimate annihilation of the Jews was clearly spelled out. Less than ten

years later Hitler was elected to the Reichstag on a political platform of anti-Semitism. His National Socialist Party (the Nazis) had never hidden their intention to rid Germany of its Jews.

It was in Paul's birth place, Meiningen in Thüringen, that Hitler was first given power, in advance of his success elsewhere. In the preface which he wrote specially for the benefit of German readers of his book, *The Double Cross*, (the German edition entitled *Aufs Kreuz gelegt)* Paul says, with stylish irony:

> *"Enthusiasm was great...even in the Church, that soon came to be numbered amongst the keenest of followers. I was not born at an auspicious time....(but) there were also spoilsports. Not many. For instance the Jews; Jews who were often proud to be German and who wanted to believe that the Führer certainly couldn't mean them. Especially those like my father who were convinced baptised Christians. But the Führer (as many realised only when it was already too late) was much too conscientious to make sentimental exceptions." (5)*

The last barrier to complete equality of opportunity and civil rights, of which Jews in Germany had been deprived for so long, was removed in 1924 when, under the Weimar Republic, they were granted equal rights to work in the civil service. Eva's father was one of those who had bene-fitted from the removal of this last barrier to equal opportunity. He held high office as a lawyer in the civil service in Munich. Eva has vivid memories of the richly cultured family life she enjoyed as a child, in which music played a central role for her from a very early age:

> *"My parents used to go to the opera about once a week. My father also led a string quartet which came to play at our house every week. Most of the people involved in these activities were university people who played or listened to music just for the enjoyment. I remember that most of my parents' friends were Jewish, but the point is that they were mostly musicians, and many of the talented musicians in Munich just happened to be*

Eva and her family: a mountaineering weekend

Jewish. It was not a conscious choice by my parents to have Jewish friends. At a very early age - perhaps two or three - I can remember humming tunes from the Mozart and Haydn quartets which I could hear wafting along the corridor to my room at night. Later on, when I was about five or six, I was allowed to stay up in my dressing gown to listen and sometimes to play short passages as second fiddle with the quartet. I've so many memories of the music. But we had other interests too. At weekends we used to go mountain climbing and skiing. They were wonderful times."

31

But the good times were not to last. When Hitler came to power in February 1933 legislation which would deprive Jews of citizenship, employment and property was rapidly introduced. The *Gesetz zur Weiderherstellung des Berufsbeamtentums,* passed on 7 April 1933, was the first of these new laws. Under it the right of Jews to employment in the civil service was removed. Civil servants were therefore the first to lose their means of livelihood. However, although for a few years Eva's family still felt fairly confident about their life in Munich because her father was on a generous pension, their long term future in Germany was already under threat, but they did not realise this until it was almost too late. Kurt's uncle also, who for many years had held a post of considerable responsibility in the civil service, lost his employment soon after the new laws were enforced.

A few months after this law was enacted, a state boycott of Jewish shops and businesses was introduced, and the number of unprovoked acts of violence against Jews increased alarmingly. No Jew, however eminent or well known, was immune from such harrassment. Sir Horace Rumbold, the British Ambassador to Berlin reported in March 1933:

> *"Today's papers state that Professor Einstein's house has been searched for explosives by SS and SA troops. Herr Bruno Walter, the celebrated conductor, was recently prevented from conducting a concert at Leipzig, and then one at Berlin, on the now classical excuse that such a proceeding on his part would result in the disturbance of public order. The house of Herr Feuchtwanger, the author, was searched by SA troops who carried away the manuscript of a novel. One of the most eminent physicians in the country, who is head of a well-known clinic, was forced to sign a paper agreeing to leave Germany. His assistants, who were also Jewish, were likewise dismissed.*
>
> *There are many instances of musicians and officials of Jewish race having been dismissed from orchestras and theatres, and in one town in Silesia the Nazis invaded the law courts and summarily forced judges and lawyers of Jewish race to cease their activities."* (6)

Kurt's father himself experienced the terror tactics which the Nazi regime was now using. At two o'clock one morning in the spring of 1934, SA troopers smashed the glass of the back door and broke into the house to 'search for weapons'. Kurt recalls:

> "My father removed the key from the door to the residential part of the house, went to the window and yelled at the top of his voice for the works manager who lived opposite, "Scheele! Scheele!" I can still hear my father shouting. I had never heard him shout like that. Scheele had the courage to come over, and only then, with Scheele as a witness, did my father open the door. This was just a typical action meant to intimidate the Jews."

If, by 1935, there were any Jews who still had confidence that there was a secure future for them in Germany, their illusions should have been shattered by the Nuremberg Laws which were passed in September of that year. These laws defined the racial doctrine and classified Jews according to their Jewish ancestry. Even someone with only one grandparent of Jewish descent was classified as non-Aryan. My sister and I, and the others in our group who had non-Jewish mothers, would have been classified as 'Mischling - erste Klasse' which can be directly (and sarcastically) translated as cross-breed - first class! Henceforth we would be referred to as non-Aryans. There could no longer be any doubt that Nazi persecution would be directed against all Jews. Whatever their status, however valuable their contribution to the German nation, they were no longer wanted in their homeland. Jewish and non-Aryan university professors, teachers, scientists, lawyers, doctors, dentists, welfare assistants and employees in commercial enterprises could now be summarily dismissed. The Jewish press was banned, and Jews and non-Aryans could no longer rely on having any protection under the law or any legal rights.

The crucial decision to leave Germany grew daily more urgent, but for most Jews this was a traumatically painful decision to make. The screw of Nazi oppression was turned with subtlety and stealth. It seemed impossible to believe that the nation to whom they had given so much would betray them. The obscene slanders of anti-semitic propaganda only slowly affected their status within the society of which they had so recently become accepted as equal and even valued citizens. The increasing isolation, discrimination, victimisation and persecution suffered by the Jewish community in Germany, and later in Nazi-occupied countries, was achieved by a cunningly timed series of oppressive dictats. After each downward turn of the screw the Jews, whose very religion encourages optimism, and trust that God will never forsake his chosen people, felt that as things stood, they could still somehow make for themselves a life worth living; that if things didn't get worse they could still somehow cope. Each time, they assumed that this latest vindictive piece of discriminatory legislation would surely be the last, and that if they cooperated no further action would be taken against them. By the time they came to realise what the end of this road might lead to, it was for most of them already too late.

To leave their homeland was to leave all that they valued most; their relatives and friends; their homes; often their professions; a language which they valued; a culture which had been their inspiration. In his auto-biography, Chaim Weizmann, leading Zionist and Professor of Chemistry at the University of Manchester, who was to become Israel's first President, quotes Richard Willstätter, the Jewish Nobel prize winning Professor of Chemistry at Munich University, as saying:

> *"I know that Germany has gone mad, but if a mother*
> *falls ill it is not a reason for her children to leave her.*
> *My home is Germany, my university, in spite of what has*
> *happened, is in Munich. I must remain."*   *(7)*

Above all, it came as a profound shock to find that their Jewish ancestry set them apart as second class citizens. Ida remembers her happy and carefree early childhood, when she and her family felt themselves to be at the heart of their community in Minden:

> *"My grandparents and my parents lived in two adjoining*
> *flats which they linked by breaking down the dividing wall,*
> *thus creating a beautiful large dining room with a balcony*
> *where we dined on special occasions. Adjacent to this*
> *was an elegantly furnished Baroque style sitting room*

*with a piano which my mother played beautifully. Each
flat retained its own bedrooms, bathroom and kitchen, so
we had both independence and togetherness with my
grandparents, and life was very pleasant for us all. Three
years after moving there my grandfather died of a heart
attack and my grandmother was then included in all our
activities and I grew very close to her.*

*My father held a very responsible position in my grand-
father's bank and was a very busy man, but when I was
little he would sometimes devote a whole afternoon to
playing wonderful games with me, like going on imagi-
nary journeys. When I was older we would go on long
cycle rides, picking mushrooms which we later made into
a delicious meal. We would look at flowers, birds and
insects which my father would point out as the wonders
of nature and he instilled in me a love for God's creation.
He was also a great sportsman, an excellent tennis player,
and it was he who taught me to skate. I remember skating
with my friends, forming a long chain with my father at
the head and me at the end, and we would cover long dis-
tances gliding over the frozen lake in the centre of our
little town."*

But Ida and her family were soon to feel the pain of being frozen out of
the community to which they had contributed so much, and they were
deeply hurt by the humiliation of their non-Jewish friends beginning to
avoid them. Nazi rules, unwillingly applied by her teachers, forced Ida
to sit isolated and alone at the back of the classroom, and she was excluded
from many school activities. Non-Jewish clients no longer consulted her
father for legal advice putting his business under severe financial strain:

*"All this should have been a sure indication that our lives
in Germany were in danger, but my parents, like millions
of other Jews, firmly believed that the inherent decency
of the German people would prevent a disaster and that
Hitler and his gang would not remain in power much
longer."*

Kurt's father also was confident that he would be protected by the loyalty of the rural community in which he had grown up, and for whom his cigar factory provided such an invaluable opportunity to earn extra income. Kurt's recollections are of an idyllic childhood home:

"My grandfather bought an old mansion - Schloss Werther - a sort of castle with a moat around it. He established a cigar factory there and when my parents married they moved into this place. It was wonderful to grow up there. We children had such fun in the gardens; when deliveries of the huge bales of tobacco arrived we used to climb all over them; we played hide and seek in the factory buildings; it was a really interesting place for a child. Next to the moat was a mill for which the the moat acted as a reservoir. At harvest time a threshing machine came to the mill, and we would go to watch. All the local farmers, and people who had a small plot of land as well as having a job, like the local blacksmith and the village carpenter, used to bring their corn to the mill to have it threshed and ground into flour. In addition, my father was able to give people from the village and from the surrounding rural area extra work rolling cigars during the winter evenings, which was a useful supplement to their meagre income as farmers. I enjoyed this life, as we all did. We felt ourselves to be truly at the heart of this community. We were a part of the village life."

"My father had grown up in Werther and thought that nothing could happen to him. Despite the fact that his twin brother, who worked for the civil service, was thrown out of his job, despite the fact that his cousin who owned a shop in Werther had had his windows smashed in and his business boycotted, my father closed his eyes and said, 'I am a manufacturer. Nothing can happen to me'."

Even the harassment he had experienced in 1934, had not dented his confidence that his future in Germany was secure.

Schloss Werther: Kurt's home until 1939

Neither did those Jews who had become Christians gain added protection from their adopted religion. Paul's father, deeply traumatised by the experience of trench warfare and national defeat, was baptised soon after the first world war. The fact that he was known to be an active Christian made no difference to people's attitude:

> "*In the mid 1930s, as my father's Jewishness became part of other people's consciousness, his practice as a paediatrician began to dwindle. People became frightened to go to a Jewish doctor. The fact that he was a Christian made no difference, as a racial concept. As far as people were concerned he was a Jew. And so he began to accept this role in a way he hadn't previously.*"

The timing of the decision to leave Germany was to be crucial to the fate of the Jewish community. For those who left early the legal formalities were comparatively straightforward, and entry to host countries, while certainly restricted because of the economic difficulties of the inter-war period, was far easier than it was to become later when a mass emigration of German Jews seemed likely. So, why did some families leave

Germany as soon as Hitler came to power - some even earlier - and why did others procrastinate until, sadly, it was too late?

Of our group, my father was one of the first to emigrate. As exports manager for his uncle's leather firm he travelled all over Europe, especially to England where he had made many friends in the trade. He realised that it would not be difficult to set up his own business here. He was also able to view the political upheavals in Germany through the eyes of his many English friends. He had great admiration for the freedom and genuine democracy, taken so much for granted in Britain, which made the harsh reality of life in Germany appear all the more sinister. In 1933 the formalities for emigration were minimal compared to the nightmare of barriers which made it so difficult for people to leave Germany by the end of the decade. Desperately sad as he was to leave his many relatives and friends, he had no difficulty in making the decision to come to Britain. Everything had been arranged by the spring of 1934. The delay caused by my father's illness, which could best be treated in Switzerland, posed no additional problems to the legal formalities of emigration. My family were able to come to England in 1936, bringing all their possessions - but no money - with them.

Renate's family left in similar circumstances. Because of his responsibility for the export side of his family lace making business, her father had spent at least half his working time in England. He was under no illusions that his conversion to Christianity would protect him from persecution in Germany. When Hitler came to power he immediately applied to move to Britain, but Renate's mother did not see the need to move at that time. The family had recently moved into their newly built home and her father's position in the family firm seemed for the time being to be secure.

> *"What finally gave my parents the push was that, because I was good at sport, I was chosen to represent the school at the Plauen Sports Rally in 1935. However, this was objected to because I was half Jewish, so I was not allowed to represent the school. This action was taken against me because of the Nuremberg Laws which had been introduced that year. We came to England just a few months later."*

Renate's family home in Jocketa, Saxony, built by her parents in 1928 in which they lived until forced to leave Germany in 1935

For businessmen, who had friends and connections overseas, and the confidence that they could establish a new enterprise in another country, such a decision was not difficult to make. But for lawyers and doctors there was the certainty that their knowledge and years of professional experience would be unrecognised outside Germany. Without studying and taking appropriate exams they could not practise their profession in another country. Luke's father nevertheless responded to the early warnings. In 1934 he gave up his law practice to come to Britain for a few months to see whether he could establish a new life here for his family. Jews could not take any money out of Germany, but until late 1937 it was possible to bring out personal possessions.

> *"He planned to run a printing factory with another Jewish friend from Germany. Erich Loerning would be the technical expert, my father the business manager; but he had to give up a very, very successful career as a lawyer in Berlin to do this."*

Having realised that he might be successful in setting up a printing company Luke's father returned to Germany. He knew that he would be prevented from taking any money with him when he emigrated, so he decided to invest his savings in his future by purchasing the most technically advanced high quality German printing presses, and equipment for photogravure, still a comparatively new technology in Britain at that time. The families came out together in 1937, bringing all the machines they needed to set up their factory in Slough.

The fathers of Ida, Eva and Ruth were also lawyers, very reluctant to lose the benefit of their years of professional experience, and therefore hesitant to leave because they were so unsure of a future for their family outside Germany. Eva's father was, moreover, lulled into a false sense of security by the generous pension he was receiving. Ruth's father did intend to emigrate, but was prevented from leaving Germany because of his feeling of responsibility for his invalid mother.

Paul's father realised that to continue to practise as a doctor in any country outside Germany he would have to take exams to re-qualify for registration. He did not react to the danger until 1938, when the threat of arrest forced the family to flee to the comparative safety of anonymity in Berlin. By then, all these parents were left in no doubt about the grave dangers which threatened their future in Germany, and were desperate to find a place of refuge. As the situation in Germany grew daily more threatening, so the regulations for emigration became more and more complicated and vindictively obstructive. Entry to other countries had meanwhile also become much more difficult. Many governments were facing their own problems of unemployment and feared that the 'flood' of Jewish refugees would become overwhelming. As Chaim Weizmann said: *"The world seemed to be divided into two parts - those places where they could not live, and those which they could not enter."* (8)

In addition there was anxiety about the loss of their homes and of all that they had worked so hard to acquire. Without financial security or the likelihood of finding suitable employment overseas the future appeared to be just as bleak and hopeless in another country as it now was in Germany. There seemed little sense in leaving the familiar, if now hostile, environment of their homeland for an uncertain future in a foreign land. The Jewish psychologist and writer, Bruno Bettelheim, who was himself a survivor of Buchenwald and Dachau recalls:

*"In Buchenwald I talked to hundreds of German Jewish
prisoners who were brought there in the fall of 1938. I
asked them why they had not left Germany because of
the utterly degrading and discriminatory conditions they
were subjected to. Their answer was: 'How could we
leave? It would have meant giving up our homes, our
places of business, everything.' Their earthly possessions had so taken possession of them that they could not
move; instead of using them, they were run by them".*

(9)

This seems a harsh judgement, but since Bettelheim was himself a victim
of Nazi persecution, and imprisoned in a concentration camp, it is a
judgement with which it would be hard to argue.

Only three families from our group had left Germany before 1938. Eve's
family in Prague were hoping that international action would save
Czechoslovakia from invasion. The other six families found themselves
still trapped in Germany on 9 November 1938. They were caught in
the full blast of the storm of Kristallnacht - the night on which the Nazis
unleashed an orchestrated campaign of terror against the Jews; "A spon-
taneous public outcry," they claimed, "In retaliation for the assassination of our diplomatic representative in Paris, Legionsrat von Rath." It
was a night which all those who experienced it are unlikely to forget.
Barry Turner sums up the brutality unleashed by the Nazis upon their
Jewish victims:

*"At around midnight the fires started. By morning 267
synagogues had been destroyed, thousands of Jewish
shops and homes devastated, one hundred Jews murdered and many thousands arrested. This was
Kristallnacht - the night of broken glass."* *(10)*

The revulsion caused by the terror of Kristallnacht, and the arrest of
30,000 Jews who were sent to concentration camps, resulted in a swing
of public opinion in Britain in favour of giving more help to refugees.
British efforts to help Jewish refugees had so far been co-ordinated by
the Central British Fund for World Jewish Relief (referred to as the

41

CBF). After Kristallnacht the rush of applications for asylum in Britain became overwhelming, so it was decided that a special effort should be made to give priority to the children. The Home Secretary at this time was Sir Samuel Hoare. He was a Quaker and had always had a special sympathy for the plight of the Jewish refugees. Now, with public opinion behind him, he at last felt able to ease the restrictions to facilitate their entry. Special travel documents would be issued in London to remove the need for children to have passports or visas. A target to save 10,000 children was suggested by the CBF; and a new co-ordinating committee, the Refugee Children's Movement, was set up to oversee this ambitious programme. Less than a week after the child refugees had been given priority status, arrangements had been made for special trains to be chartered to bring them to the Hook of Holland, and then by ferry to Britain. In Britain offers of help to care for these children were generous, both from organisations such as Jewish Welfare groups, Church groups and the Quakers, and also from private individuals. The rescue of the children, which became known as the Kindertransports, required meticulous organisation involving the total commitment of many dedicated people. By their efforts 9,354 children (as recorded in the CBF archives) were saved. Among them were Frank, Eve, Ruth and her brother, and Kurt and his brother and sisters.

On Kristallnacht, Ida was in Berlin. The atrocities of the night before left the Jewish community in the city numb with shock. Anxious because the daily letter from her father had not arrived she phoned her home to find everything in utter chaos. Her father had been arrested during the night and sent to a concentration camp. Her mother was on her way to Berlin to implore Cunard White Star, for whom Ida's father had been an agent, to help. Relatives in US, Argentina and Brazil had for months been trying to obtain visas for Ida's family. All the effort was in vain. Only Ida was able to escape. A family friend had managed to obtain a traineeship for her at a factory in Birmingham, which gave her right of entry to Britain. She left Germany on 20 June 1939, determined to find a way of bringing her parents over when she arrived here. Sadly it was already too late.

Kurt also was away from home on Kristallnacht, living in Frankfurt where he attended the Jewish school. He can remember seeing the synagogues on fire, and the general feeling of panic and terror of that night. His father was arrested and sent to Buchenwald. The torture and deprivation he suffered during the five weeks he was imprisoned resulted in a severe mental breakdown that confined him to a mental hospital until he and his wife were at last able to emigrate to Britain. He had already been forced to 'transfer' his cigar factory to an 'Aryan' competitor who owned factories in a nearby town, leaving the family in severe financial difficulties. Kurt's mother was left to cope on her own with the appalling nightmare of *Auswanderung* (emigration) and with the pain of parting with her children as they left Germany on the Kindertransport; Kurt's older brother in February 1939, his twin sisters in April, and Kurt in May. Kurt comments poignantly:

> "*The thought of a mother taking her children to the station, not knowing if she would ever see them again; no address; husband in hospital; having to prepare the emigration all by herself. Just try to put yourself into that picture. And my mother just did it.*"

When the affidavits came through for his parents to come to Britain too, permission for Kurt's paternal grandmother had been refused, adding further to the acute anxiety from which his father was already suffering. They left Germany, almost at the last moment, at the end of August 1939.

Frank and his parents, who were well known and well liked in their home community of Dachau, had personally experienced no unpleasantness or persecution up to this time. As far as Frank can remember, there was only one other Jewish family in the town and all his friendships as a young child were with non-Jewish children who lived nearby.

But suddenly everything changed. Following the assassination of the German diplomat Legionsrat von Rath in Paris, the fervour of hatred against Jews had been deliberately fomented by the regime. Fear and tension made itself felt even in the hitherto friendly community of Frank's home town. His parents' closest friends, who lived in Munich, were planning to leave the city for the comparative safety of the countryside. Here they themselves had very good friends, the Schneblinger family,

who owned a farm in the tiny village of Ruhpolding in the Bavarian Alps. Herr Schneblinger was a courageously outspoken anti-Nazi. Sensing his friends' fear and unease in the prevailing anti-semitic mood, he suggested that they should come to stay at his farm until the immediate crisis was over, and he invited them to bring Frank and his parents too. Frank recalls:

Frank on the left aged about five, with one of his friends

"On Kristallnacht everything changed. We had to leave our house suddenly, over-night and we never returned to it. I couldn't go to school again after that. It was a complete break with the past, because after that we felt under constant threat; there was absolutely no feeling of security. We knew that we no longer had any place in Germany. There was no future for us here. My uncles, who had already left Germany by then, and a cousin who had emigrated to the US much earlier, were trying desperately to get us out. My parents, who had applied for visas to various countries rather too late, were still hoping to leave."

At the end of July 1939, after nine months of tension and anxiety, during which he lived with his mother's sister in Paderborn, Frank was able to leave Germany on the Kindertransport. For his parents it was sadly too late.

Herr Schneblinger continued his courageous protest against the Nazi regime throughout the war. He certainly put his own life at risk by his actions, and his family lived in great danger. There was the constant threat of imprisonment, but they never wavered in their opposition to Hitler's brutal regime. Fortunately they survived these terrifying years and, a few years after the war, Frank took his family to visit them; indeed he had the great joy of introducing his own children to Herr Schneblinger's grandchildren; and as a teenager, his oldest daughter, Catherine, spent a summer holiday with them.

Eva woke on the morning of 10 November to find that her father had been arrested during the night. Later that day SA troopers came back, terrorising the family and demanding that they should be at the frontier by six o'clock that evening. The trauma of those events has haunted her ever since, with the result that the memory of what happened from that day, until the return of her father some five weeks later, has been completely blocked out of her mind.

> *"My father was taken to Dachau. He was diabetic. Without insulin or adequate food he was just skin and bone, literally a walking skeleton when he came out, and he was in hospital for a whole month. Up to that time he couldn't believe that people like him, who had worked for Germany, had fought for Germany, could be persecuted. He had always said, 'Nothing can happen to us, I have my pension. They won't touch me.' But after Dachau he said, 'Not one more hour. Even if I have got nothing, not one more second than necessary.' The next four months were hell. Every day to another office to get a stamp on a piece of paper. The whole of life became, 'How long? How long? How long?'"*

Paul's last few months in Germany were spent in hiding in Berlin. His parents were fully occupied in trying to find a way out. Eventually a medical friend of Paul's father, who had already emigrated to New Zealand, offered to be a guarantor. But entry to New Zealand was notoriously difficult. Two guarantors were needed, and in addition refugees were required to bring in £100 each, a huge sum of money in those days. It would take time to sort out all these difficulties. Meanwhile Paul's mother visited him when she could, to take him for a walk. She did that on the day that turned out to be Kristallnacht. It was a seminal experience for Paul. Although he didn't understand his own role in the violence

*Paul Oestreicher and his father, Dr Paul Oestreicher, during the months
'on the run' in Berlin (his father wearing his Iron Crosses won during
World War I which gave him some measure of temporary protection)*

which he witnessed all around him, he realised that he was in some way
affected by it. He recalls:

> *"My mother grew tense. Lorries stopped at intervals by
> the roadside, filled with black uniformed men. A whistle
> blew and they jumped down and were suddenly all round
> us, swinging great truncheons and smashing up the shop
> fronts. Sudden terror and broken glass all round us.
> Jewish shops. We got away quickly, physically unharmed.
> But the damage had been done. Though my parents had*

tried to shelter me from the truth, I knew in my bones, this
was not about THEM, this was about US."   *(11)*

With the help of the office of the courageous Lutheran pastor, Heinrich
Grüber, a second guarantor was found through the Anglican Church of
New Zealand.   Heinrich Grüber was eventually arrested himself and
imprisoned in a concentration camp for his part in helping the Jews; he
survived and after the war was appointed Provost of Berlin.   The money
required for entry to New Zealand was donated to Paul's father by a complete stranger, the friend of a distant relative, who hearing of their predica-
ment sent them the sum needed:

> *"We have always said that to this unknown Frenchman*
> *we owe our lives.   By the time war was ended he had*
> *died, but we did meet his widow who said - 'This is the*
> *sort of opportunity that made my husband proud to be*
> *a human being.' "*

On leaving Germany, Paul's father reacted to the obstructive regulations
with the same positive commonsense as had Luke's father. With courage
and humour he took the opportunity of one last small act of revenge
against the brutal Nazi regime.

> *"People who had won Iron Crosses in the First World War*
> *were put into a category of Jews that were permitted, once*
> *they had obtained a visa to another country, to take with*
> *them all they possessed except their money!   By 1938 the*
> *only purpose for which they could use their money was to*
> *buy a one way ticket out of Germany from the Reiseburo.*
> *But it did not state in the regulations, 'by the cheapest*
> *means possible'.   So my father booked State Class in a*
> *luxury liner. 'That much money we'll take out of Hitler's*
> *coffers!'   So we poor penniless refugees travelled like*
> *millionaires to New Zealand, and took all our family*
> *heirlooms with us."*

Paul still treasures the paintings which belonged to his grandmother.
And so it was that in the late spring of 1939 Paul and his parents said a
sad farewell to Germany, and set sail for a new life.

Eve remembers clearly the sudden change in her family life after the invasion of Czechoslovakia in March 1939. There was a feeling of fear and tension, and she knew that she had to keep quiet to avoid drawing any attention to herself because she was Jewish. The Kindertransport was started almost at once from Prague, and Eve's parents made arrangements for her and her brother to be fostered in Britain.

The schedules were arranged for the youngest to leave first, and Eve left her family on July 1st. Her brother was due to leave on September 3rd - the very day that war broke out. No more Kindertransports could leave. Eve never saw her brother or her parents again. Of her many relations only one uncle and aunt, and two cousins survived.

Eve and her brother at a family swimming party: Eve's mother is behind her wearing a head scarf

Ruth has only scanty memories of her life before she left Germany. She knows that her father was on a 'wanted' list, probably because of the nature of his work as a lawyer. To avoid arrest he spent a lot of time away from home, often taking Martin, Ruth's older brother with him. He wanted to take the family to a safe refuge abroad, but could not leave Germany because of the responsibility he felt for his invalid mother. However arrangements were made for Ruth and her brother to leave Germany on the Kindertransport. Because she was so young, Ruth and her brother were brought to Britain to their first foster home by their mother, who was then obliged by the regulations governing the running of the Kindertransports, to return immediately to Germany.

Ruth's mother, not being Jewish, was relatively safe living in Berlin during the war, and her security was further enhanced by being parted from her Jewish husband when he was able to emigrate. He had stayed in Germany until the death of his mother in May 1939, but managed at the last moment to escape to Shanghai.

These circumstances resulted in very different experiences for us as children both before and during the war. For Renate and Luke, and for me, the move to England was relatively calm and untroubled. We came with our family to an already established circle of friends who gave support and encouragement to our parents. They had the certainty of a livelihood, albeit involving extremely hard work and commitment. Naturally they felt deeply the sorrow of leaving behind friends and relatives about whom there was great anxiety, but the decision to come had been made all the easier for having been taken so early.

For the other seven families in our group the decisions were far less clear, far more difficult, more harrowing to make. They had more to lose by leaving Germany; professions or businesses that would be almost

Ruth aged 3: a few months before leaving Berlin on the Kindertransport

impossible to rebuild in a foreign land; few friends or contacts outside Germany; the insecurity of not knowing whether they could provide adequately for their families. By the outbreak of war we were already well settled and the process of integration into the British way of life was well in hand. For the others the personal experience of brutal persecution, of fear, of witnessing parents driven to despair, of the terrifying anxiety of those last months of trying to find a way out, left an indelible mark. Eva, and eventually Kurt, had the security of having their family here. But only a few weeks after their arrival war broke out. They were abruptly cut off from all they had known. They carried with them the memories of what had been, until Hitler came to power, an idyllic early childhood. Now an iron gate clanged shut on that former life. Another life in another country was about to begin.

IN MEMORIAM

Memorial to the victims of the Holocaust in Teresienstadt

Ida's parents, and many of her close relatives and friends.

Two aunts of Renate. One aunt, headmistress of a Jewish Girls' School, had all formalities for emigration completed and could have left at any time, but refused to abandon her pupils until all were safe. She perished with those who could not escape.

Frank's parents, and many close relatives and friends.

Kurt's grandmother, uncle and cousin, and many friends.

Eva's grandmother, Phillipine.

Eve's parents, brother and most of her many close relatives and friends.

Paul's grandmother, who took her own life on the night before she was due to report for deportation. She wrote: *"...A brave captain does not abandon his sinking ship..."*

Luke's grandmother.

My grandparents and many of my father's close relatives and friends.

50

ALL THE LEAVES HAVE LOST THEIR TREES
(For Hannah who said it)

All the leaves have lost their trees.
Child, what tumbled words are these?
(Yet I grieve for my lost tree:
Far away the wind bore me.)

Gerda Mayer   (12)

Reprinted by kind permission of Gerda Mayer from Bernini's Cat
(New and Selected Poems) by Gerda Mayer, Iron Press, 1999

One effect of Nazi policy towards the Jews was to awaken what for many
Jews in Germany (and in neighbouring countries) had become a latent
sense of their own Jewishness. Paul describes this effect in a very personal way when he comments that because of the change in attitude of
patients and friends, who began to avoid and eventually to desert him, his
father was forced to *"...accept this role (being a Jew) in a way he had not
done before".* When the Nuremberg laws were proclaimed in 1935:

> *"...the racial doctrine became well defined. Before, it had*
> *been expressed in violent clashes, hysterical speeches,*
> *lurid newspaper articles; now it became legal as well as*
> *'scientific' law."*   *(13)*

The degree of Jewishness was defined in these laws, and those with non-
Jewish as well as Jewish parents or grandparents were classified as non-
Aryan. This made it possible to apply restrictive legislation to Jews and
non-Aryans only. They could be isolated from the rest of the German
population; disenfranchised; deprived of the right to practise their profession; cast outside the normal protection of the law. But it also
reminded them of their Jewish heredity. Their sense of national identity was damaged, if not immediately destroyed. They were not, as they
had thought, Germans who happened to be Jewish. They were Jews
who happened (unfortunately) to live in Germany.

For those refugee children old enough to remember the persecution which they and their families suffered in the late 1930s, this self-identification as being Jewish was to become a source of strength. Five of our group of ten, - Ida, Renate, Frank, Kurt and Eva - were over the age of twelve when they came to Britain. The rest, - Eve, Paul, Ruth, Luke and I - were under eight when we left. We younger ones had little sense of self-identity, of who we were, of what group or groups we belonged to, of what our place in society might be. This personal awareness had yet to develop. The older children were well aware of who they were before they came to Britain.

Renate was twelve when her family came to live in London, sixteen when war was declared; old enough to understand the reasons why her family had left Germany, and the nature of the threat against the Jews who still lived in Germany. Renate's mother, not being Jewish, could return to Germany safely to keep in touch with her family, taking Renate and her sister for holidays until the summer of 1939.

Because of these links Renate could see for herself that, depraved as the regime was, not all Germans were Nazis. The reports of the atrocities of Kristallnacht came as a terrible shock. Applications were made

Renate and her sister on a holiday visit to their grandmother in Germany in the late 1930s

immediately for her Jewish grandmother to come out, and within a fortnight Renate's mother had gone back to Germany to escort her mother-in-law to safety in Britain. Renate's father helped many people to escape by finding British guarantors and by providing board and lodging in the family home until the newcomers were able to arrange their own accommodation. He also helped to reorganise the filing of documents at Bloomsbury House, where applications for entry to Britain were processed, thereby improving speed and efficiency at a time when the system was near breaking point by the sheer number of requests for help.   As he said, *"Every file lost is a life lost."* Renate was therefore well informed and aware of the danger that could have threatened her family.   Her Jewish roots, however, were not of great significance to her own self-identity, nor to the ethos of her family life.   She had a very clear image of two Germanys; the Germany of her mother's family and others like them and the Germany of Hitler and the Nazis.   She knew to which she belonged.

Frank was only fifteen when he came to Britain, but already had a strong sense of identity as is clear from his account of his early years here:

> *"The Church of England Committee for Refugees,(who sponsored me) very kindly, I suppose, sent me to Monkton Combe School in the autumn of 1939 and I had two extremely miserable terms there, partly because it was very cold.   The regime was extremely austere and the winter of 1939/40 was particularly severe.   Also I was subjected to an absolute barrage of attempts to convert me to Christianity.   Help arrived in a rather unexpected way when the Admiralty moved to Bath in May 1940. Because, technically, I was an enemy alien, and might have endangered the future of the Armed Forces, I had to be removed!   So I was sent to Dean Close School in Cheltenham, which was a slightly more relaxed regime.*
>
> *I had very little trouble deciding what my identity was because Monkton Combe managed to make me more aware than ever of my Jewish background, simply because they worked on me so ruthlessly.   I could say to them with a perfectly clear conscience that I could never agree to being forcibly converted without my parents' consent.   In any case I didn't want to be converted."*

The refugee hostel where, some years later, Frank and Ida met, had a comfortably familiar German Jewish ambience.   They felt at ease with the other people lodging there, who had all suffered a very similar fate, so there was a network of mutual comfort and support, and further affirmation of their sense of identity in belonging to that group.   The English people they met were very tolerant and supportive.   *"We were never*

made to feel that we were 'exotic foreigners' or different in any way."
However, Frank adds:

> *"I would never deny my origin and I am perfectly happy
> to tell people exactly how I happen to be here. This is
> a more comfortable state than writing off a whole part
> of one's existence by denying a certain part of what is
> essentially very much part of one's personality."*

Kurt also arrived in Britain with a developed sense of self-identity, but
he met with a very different attitude from his school to the one Frank
had had to endure. On his first morning he was met at the school gate
by another Jewish pupil of his own age who had been selected to be his
guide and friend for the first few weeks - a thoughtful gesture which,
Kurt says, was typical of the Headmaster, Alex Crombie. It was his
personal generosity which enabled Kurt to remain as a boarder when the
school was evacuated to Cornwall. Kurt's school experience was a very
happy introduction to his new life in Britain:

> *"England was heaven after all I had experienced in
> Germany. It was for me like a convalescence. I loved
> the countryside, and for the first time I was given some
> responsibility....I organised salvage collections from dif-
> ferent farms. At the end I had the whole of West Cornwall
> under my control! The Cornish farmers were a help to
> me personally too. The advantage I had there, in
> Cornwall, was that anyone who was not Cornish was a
> foreigner. So the English boys were foreigners just as
> much as I was."*

For Eva's family liberal Jewish traditions remained as the core of a loving
family life, and her confidence was strengthened by the supportive and
friendly ethos of her primary school:

> *"I was amused to be in this school where I couldn't
> understand a word! But I seemed to make friends very
> quickly, you know, how children do. It took me only
> about four weeks before I could understand everything,
> and everyone was terribly kind and helpful. I came*

home saying, 'You know, they don't seem to mind that I'm Jewish. I can't believe it.' I was very happy."

Revealed in this innocent comment is the depth of negative expectation which Eva had developed as a result of the persecution she had suffered during her last few years in Germany. She remembers a typical experience of how afraid she had become of breaking the discriminatory rules governing even the most innocent of leisure activities of the Jewish community:

Eva - for whose family music was a solace

"I used to adore skating. There was a big skating rink just behind my home, and I remember very clearly how my mother used to say, 'Now, just remember that it says - Juden unerwünscht (Jews not welcome). So don't do anything to cause a disturbance. Be a good girl, and you'll be alright.' And I remember sort of hesitating, and saying, 'Are you sure?' and her reply, 'Yes, of course... you'll be alright.' So off I'd go. I must have been about eight or nine, and I know I used to wonder what would happen if they found out that I was Jewish, and there was a sort of fear about going skating. But then I'd put my skates on; and as soon as I started to skate I'd forget all the fear because I just enjoyed it so much."

55

Eva's Jewish heredity had become a burden, and yet the family observance of religious tradition was a source of great comfort and strength:

"As things got worse and worse in Germany the tension communicated itself, whether one understood it or not. You could tell...it was a non-security, angst perhaps, real angst. I can remember that for the one second my father placed his hands on my head, every Friday night, it made me feel safe. It was a wonderful feeling. And we used to do it in England too, of course, and I had this feeling of reassurance and relief, although I never really needed it then. What a great thing that was for the family."

In spite of all they had experienced, all five of this older group retained a strong sense of self-worth which was, if anything, strengthened by their experience in Britain. While her father's Jewish roots were not of particular significance to Renate's family life, his commitment to helping Jewish refugees left a deep impression on her. Ida, Frank, Kurt and Eva were already committed to their Jewish identity when they came to Britain and although Eva had negative expectations of other people's attitudes, her pride in being Jewish never deserted her. For all of them it proved to be a source of strength.

Those of us who came to Britain at a younger age developed our sense of identity here in our new homeland. We were very vulnerable, and dependent on the influence of those around us, of our parents and of those 'in loco parentis'. We were sensitive to peer pressure and to what other children would think of us. It was natural that we were identified as 'the enemy', or at least as foreign, and therefore as legitimate targets of suspicion. This added a dimension of tension and anxiety which, for some of us, confused our sense of identity and lowered our self esteem.

Eve's parents were not practising Jews, so she had no experience of Jewish traditions or religious ceremonies. She arrived in Britain with no understanding of what it meant to be Jewish. During the last few months of her life in Prague she had felt the fear and anxiety of her parents and their friends, and had learnt to associate their increasing despair with their Jewish identity. Clearly one had to keep quiet about being Jewish.

The long experience Eve's foster mother had had of working with young children enabled her to understand the emotional turmoil which engulfed her eight year old ward during her first few weeks here. She gave Eve affection, time to sort out her feelings, and patient gentle care. It was not long before close bonds developed between them:

> "After the excitement of the first week or so, I really began to miss my family. But I soon became very close to my new Mum. I really loved her; so much so that I began to worry about what would happen after the war. I realised that I might have two lots of parents and I didn't want to leave this one because I had grown to love her so much. During the first year or so I felt a bit of an outsider, specially at primary school where the children were either really horrid because I wasn't English or over-protective because I was a refugee. So I did feel 'different'. But I soon felt that my real life and my real friends were here in the Midlands. Later I went to a small, very friendly girls' grammar school where everybody knew I was Czech, but by now I was quite proud of it. They didn't know I was Jewish...necessarily. I kept that very, very secret, because I was afraid. I just knew that if you were Jewish, and people knew you were Jewish, you had reason to be afraid."

It is not surprising that Eve wanted to become totally integrated into the friendly community in which she was growing up. She longed to be exactly the same as her friends, and to be accepted as such by them. Her Jewish background was part of that other life in Prague which no longer seemed real:

> "I never took any interest in my Jewish background, or met other Jewish people. I think that my Jewish origin is now completely irrelevant to my personality and my life."

Ruth and her brother were not so fortunate. Ruth believes that she and her brother were sponsored by the Quakers to come to England, but their first few years in Britain were very unsettled and disturbed. Their first foster parents were a well meaning Rector, and his wife. She was motivated by duty rather than by genuine tenderness or understanding in the care of her young wards. She imposed a strict regime of rules, and punishments for minor misdemeanours. Four year old Ruth was starved of the affection and reassurance she craved and needed. In her unhappiness she wet her bed, which was only to be expected. For this she was strapped. She was deprived of food for not behaving correctly at table, or for not speaking English properly. Her brother risked punishment himself by raiding the larder at night to feed her:

> *"In a way my brother became my mother. He kept me alive, literally; physically by feeding me and psychologically because he was the one thing that stayed the same. Everything else vanished. I became tremendously dependent on him. And he on me. He remembers the last words from our parents were, 'Look after your little sister.' So that I was his 'raison d'etre'. He couldn't let go. He couldn't give up. He had to look after me. That was his link with our parents. We were taken to church every Sunday and I began to understand what 'church' and 'religion' were all supposed to be about. All this 'goodness' and 'kindness' and 'love one another'. I picked up the hypocrisy of what was said in church compared to what happened at home. That really turned me against religion."*

Within the first five years of their life in England Ruth and her brother lived in five different 'homes'. Once again, Ruth had reason to be grateful to Quakers, for her first experience of security and happiness in her new life in England came when she and her brother were sent from the Rectory to board at the Friends' School in Saffron Walden. Ruth remembers the love and understanding care which the children here were given, and the reawakening of her self confidence as a result - such was the contrast to the harsh regime she had come to expect as 'normal' at the Rectory. It was a particularly happy and carefree time, but sadly short-lived; for after only two years at Friends' School, Ruth's guardian, the Rector, became ill and could no longer take responsibility for his two young

Ruth on the farm

wards. They had to leave the school and never returned to the Rectory, being sent instead to a hostel in Richmond, and from there to a second and then to a third foster home. Here at last, in the loving but disciplined family life, and the companionship of other children, Ruth found the security and affection she needed.

"I can remember very well going to this farm and being absolutely enchanted by the animals. There was a sort of safe freedom to the family life here. Everything was very well organised, and yet there was the freedom to do all sorts of things with the animals. I liked it so much that I was absolutely determined that this time I wasn't going to be 'thrown out' again. I tackled that problem by being over-willing to take on chores in the hope that I would become indispensible! I mean - I hated washing up and I hated cleaning - but I just forced myself to do it, so I suppose it wasn't really all that willing! However, all the things I had to do on the farm were tasks I wanted to do and I never could have enough of that - I enjoyed it so much. I was allowed to lead the horses hauling the full hay wagons home, and later learnt to drive the

*empty wagons out to the fields and helped to stack the
sheaves of corn. I worked the horses and looked after
other farm animals. It was quite strenuous and
demanding but it didn't seem like work to me!*

*I was also allowed to have my own animals. I had some
rabbits, and later I had pigs of my own, and a pony. I
so idealised this life with my foster parents that I decided
that one day I would have a farm of my own."*

But the unhappy instability of those first five years left their mark. With
such frequent changes of home it was impossible for Ruth and her brother
to develop any sense of identity. They seemed to belong nowhere and
to nobody because they were always being moved on. Ruth's self-worth
was constantly challenged by feeling that she had been rejected; first by
her own parents, then by her first foster parents, by school and by the
hostel, and then by the second foster parents before finding a safe haven
with her fourth set of parents. In addition, like most of us, she was
harassed and teased for being German, though the brief period at Friends'
School was a happy exception to this hurtful experience. She defended
herself against this playground bullying by building up her Jewish
identity:

*"I replied that I couldn't be German. I had been kicked
out of Germany because I wasn't German. I had had
to leave because I was Jewish. So I developed a Jewish
identity without having a clue really as to what being
Jewish meant."*

Ruth suffered deep insecurity for many years. Self-esteem and a clear
sense of identity did not develop until she met her future husband at university. He is British and, to her joyful surprise, came from a Jewish
family, though he had not been brought up in the faith. After their marriage Ruth and her husband 'discovered' Judaism together, and the Reform
Jewish tradition became the core of their richly rewarding family life.

Luke was about the same age as Ruth - four - when war was declared,
and like her, was still at primary school when it ended. He was fortunate

in living at home with his parents during these impressionable years. They wanted their children to assimilate as quickly as possible into the life of their community, but Jewish traditions remained as the basis for family life. Luke went to synagogue with his father, but was encouraged to have a very open-minded liberal attitude to other religions, and he was not discouraged from also going to church with his school friends if he wished to do so. Luke's father was very interested in all religions:

> *"My father was quite drawn to the Christian ethic and he knew a great deal about the coming together of the religions. He was not at all protective that we should all do one thing or the other. When I went to Cambridge I was influenced by the fairly religious 'monastic' life at Jesus College, and I became confirmed, but I have always felt Jewish in its racial sense, and we continued sometimes with some of the Jewish festivals."*

Luke has never felt that his Jewish identity prevented him from feeling completely at home and integrated into life here. At his secondary school, St Paul's, there were many other Jewish pupils, so his Jewish identity was affirmed. After his conversion to Christianity he had no difficulty in accommodating a dual loyalty to both aspects of his personality.

Refugees were greeted with considerable hostility in New Zealand, so Paul's parents needed courage and determination to come to terms with their new life. The high level of unemployment was used by the New Zealand government as the official excuse to resist pressure from the British government to relax its restrictive immigration rules. Strong protectionist barriers were set up by the New Zealand Medical Council to prevent refugee doctors from 'threatening' the status of New Zealand born and educated doctors. A full-time three-year clinical study to re-qualify was compulsory (in what was after all, at least for some months, a foreign language). Paul's father sometimes referred to this as his 'academic concentration camp'. He completed this successfully, but was one of very few doctors able to face this extremely daunting challenge.

As committed Christians who became Quakers in New Zealand, Paul's parents integrated well into the local community through involvement in the life of the Society of Friends. However they were also determined that they would not reject their German identity. This was an important affirmation of Paul's self-esteem, because he absorbed the admiration which his parents had for German culture:

> "My parents said, 'There is another Germany which we stand for and we are to be its ambassadors.' One of the results was that we spoke only German in our household except when we had English speaking visitors. I was very embarrassed as a child, but I grew up totally bilingual. My parents took German culture with them and maintained it and our home became a sort of cultural enclave which many New Zealanders came to appreciate."

Paul's mother continued to delight audiences, singing Bach cantatas and arias, and lieder by Schubert and Schumann, Brahms and Wolf. She also played the piano, and developed her knowledge of European folk art, painting their furniture in the style of German peasant art. His father encouraged an interest in German literature and poetry. Paul's home had the ambience of the best of German artistic creativity. He had every reason to grow up taking pride in the cultural heritage of his native land.

Like most of us Paul was teased and bullied in the playground, but he resisted the anti-German taunts by taking the line that it was 'special' to be a refugee:

> "Undoubtedly it is a bit of my personality to put up a strong resistance. I was influenced by my parents who kept saying, 'You have nothing to be ashamed of.' They always brought out the good sides of German culture and all its strengths and the good things which one stood for against the evil things Hitler was doing."

As for myself, had I lived with my parents during the crucial years of developing from childhood to adolescence I might have developed a similar appreciation of the positive aspects of my German roots. My parents had brought quite a library of German literature with them, but it remained closed for me because I lost my use of the language long before I could read the books. They were enthusiastic supporters of London's concert and theatre life, and my mother was a very good pianist and particularly enjoyed playing Beethoven sonatas, Schubert and Schumann. Certainly it is unlikely that I would have rejected my origins as ruthlessly as I did; but for the very best of reasons my parents worked hard for us to become assimilated as quickly as possible. I recall clearly my first breakfast in my new home. My sister and parents had lived in England for some months and were already speaking English fluently. I was dismayed when I was, as I thought, deliberately excluded from their conversation. But my father was uncompromising. He refused to understand my German! As a result of this policy I did learn English almost overnight, for I cannot remember ever again being unable to express myself freely. However, I also learned to regard the German language as 'disapproved of', and, as I rejected the language, so I rejected everything of German origin with it. In retrospect I often wonder whether, for our own safety, our parents 'played down' our German Jewish heredity. I was not aware of being half Jewish because this was never a part of our home life, and soon after my arrival in London my sister and I started to attend Sunday school and a few months later we were baptised.

In 1940, when an invasion seemed threateningly possible, we were sent to boarding school in the safety of the Malvern Hills. Our father was interned for some months, although we did not know about this at the time, and we did not return to our London home for about two years. During this time school became more and more important as the guiding influence. It was natural that from all that I learned, both inside and outside the classroom, one message came through. Britain stood for Democracy, Justice, Freedom and Truth, and for Being a Good Sport. She had given the world Shakespeare, Jane Austen, Dickens, great poetry and railways. Germany stood for Dictatorship, Persecution, and War, and had given the world bombed cities and nothing but misery.

It is no wonder that I was ashamed of my origins and longed desperately to be English like all my friends. It took me a lifetime of gradual adjustment to understand the depth of my prejudice against myself. I had done exactly what Frank warned against, namely I had written off *'a whole part of my existence by denying a certain part of what is essentially very much part of one's personality.'*

During these sometimes difficult school years a positive and cheering influence came into my life when I was aged 13 with the arrival of a new girl. I can still see Emma smiling as she came for the first time into our class recreation room. A very close friendship soon developed which has remained a special relationship throughout my life. Many were the happy school holidays we spent together; she in our home, or I with her family in the Quaker village of Jordans, where I attended a Quaker Meeting for the first time, although it was to be more than forty years before I became a member of the society. Through our friendship our parents came to know each other. My father and Emma's had a similar outlook on life and enjoyed long conversations about international affairs; our mothers were music enthusiasts; there was so much common ground that a firm friendship developed between them at a time, towards the end of the war, when their

Dorothy - a typical English public schoolgirl

support was a very real comfort to my parents. This friendship was to be of crucial importance to my father in the months after the war.

It is interesting to survey these varied experiences in the light of what we now know about child psychology and the crucial importance of building a child's self-esteem and affirming a positive sense of self-identity. What, I wonder, would a present-day child psychologist say of the headteacher of the junior house of our boarding school, who reprimanded me for that most popular of all boarding school crimes, 'talking after lights out', by saying - "I am just writing a letter to your mother, and I will have to tell her that you are behaving like a little Hun." To a child of nine, whose self-esteem was already near rock bottom, that spiteful remark cut deep. It left me with a loathing of my German origin and a lifelong need to 'prove' myself, to show that I am not 'a little Hun'. Unlike those children who had a sense of their Jewishness, and were proud of their heritage, I had no escape from the guilt and shame of being German. Today's child guidance experts would also have condemned as outrageous the attempts of Monkton Combe School to undermine Frank's belief in his Jewish heritage, and would have applauded the sensitivity of Alex Crombie in affirming Kurt's identity by choosing a helpful Jewish classmate to befriend him during those first few confusing weeks at his new school in England. But there was no great belief then in encouraging an obsession with our own problems! We were just expected to get on with life, whatever the circumstances, and to make the most of the opportunities that came our way. And that, precisely, is what we did.

We ten have all experienced what it feels like to be an outsider, but we are confident now of our identity as *'British first and foremost'*. Ida sums this up well for all of us:

> *"We felt utterly betrayed by Germany. Here it has been a gradual process of becoming more and more Anglicised. When I came here the difference between the subdued German people and the free English people was amazing. And that is one of the reasons why I love the English people. I don't have any divided loyalty. I belong to this country, where I can practise my religion as much or as little as I choose."*

RACE

When I returned to my home town
believing that no one would care
who I was or what I thought
it was as if the people caught
an echo of me everywhere
they knew my story by my face
and I who am always alone
became a symbol of my race

Like every living Jew I have
in imagination seen
the gas-chambers the mass grave
the unknown body which was mine
and found in every German face
behind the mask the mark of Cain
I will not make their thoughts my own
by hating people for their race.

Karen Gershon

Reproduced by kind permission of Macmillan Press
from *We Came As Children* edited by Karen Gershon
Papermac 1989   (14)

RECONCILIATION - GERMANY

In the Spring of 1994 the film *Schindler's List* was making the headlines. Everyone was talking about it, and not simply because it had been awarded seven Oscars. The story it tells is about a very ordinary human being, blackmarket racketeer, womaniser and Nazi Party member, who dared to defy the system, challenging 'The Final Solution' by rescuing 1,100 Jews from certain death. Though the film leaves many questions unanswered, it reminded people of the Holocaust and of the unimaginable depths of depravity to which ordinary human beings can fall. Equally, Schindler's story tells us that ordinary human beings can be galvanized to perform acts of courage on behalf of the weak and the oppressed quite out of character with what their previous record might suggest. Whatever his motives, Schindler was recognised by the only people whose opinion matters, by those he rescued, as a hero and as their saviour. Steve Crawshaw, who was at the time of its release the film critic for *The Independent*, reported that in Germany, watching *Schindler's List* was a traumatic event which would probably be talked about for years:

> *"For Germans....the film is perceived as an extraordinarily painful confrontation with their own country's past. I have never seen an audience so devastated by a cinema performance. As the film ended nobody moved. When they finally did, there were still tears in their eyes....In the packed Hamburg cinema there was scarcely a member of the audience old enough to have lived through the Nazi era. Their grandparents are still not keen to ask the question, 'How and why did we allow this to happen?' By contrast, the younger generations are eager to understand precisely in order to ensure that it cannot be repeated."*   *(15)*

For everyone in our group there is a certain unease and ambivalence in our relationship with the land of our birth. When we visit Germany we are aware that some of those we meet were active supporters of the Nazi regime. Others are equally implicated by their failure to oppose. The younger generation feel that they carry the burden of guilt for what their parents and grandparents did, and also for what they did not do. They ask why so few people stood up for the Jews, or dared to help them. In Yad Vashem, the memorial in Jerusalem for victims of the Holocaust, 10,000 trees were planted to commemorate those who had had the courage to help: 'The Just Among Peoples'. Only 250 trees bear the names of German citizens; one of them Schindler's; another that of Provost Heinrich Grüber of Berlin, whose work on behalf of Jewish Christians had been so crucial to the safe emigration of Paul and his parents, amongst others. The question mark lies like a barrier between us and the older German generation, but with younger Germans there is reconciliation.

Those of our parents who were not Jewish seem to have been most deeply embittered by Germany's betrayal of their Jewish husbands. Both Renate and Paul spoke of this. Renate said:

> *"My mother was more anti-German than I was. When she went there in 1938 she just couldn't understand them any more. She wrote to us saying, 'I simply don't know what is going on here and I can't understand what people are thinking of. As far as I am concerned they all speak Chinese!' I don't think my father ever had any real hatred for Germany."*

Paul's parents deeply missed the cultural life they had enjoyed in Germany. His father was quite eager to live in Germany again after the war, but his mother had felt the injustice of their enforced exile too keenly. To add even more bitterness to her dismay at the atrocities committed in the name of the nation she loved, her brother had been a high-ranking Nazi official, Head of Personnel in the Foreign Organization of the Party, (Personalleiter des Auslandsorganisation) NSDAP, - a totally divided German family. For her there was no possibility of return. Reconciliation was easier for Paul's father who often talked of the grace bestowed on him by having been born a Jew. *"How otherwise,"* he would ask, *"could one know for certain that one would not also have been a persecutor? How much better to bear a victim's pain than the oppressor's burden of guilt."*

My father returned to Germany, on his own, as soon as he was allowed to do so after the war, to find news of his parents. When my mother heard of their death she was distraught, and felt in some way personally guilty about what the Nazi regime had done in the name of the German nation. Moreoever she was uneasy about the ambiguous role played by some members of her own family. Her relationship with Germany and even with some of her own close relatives remained strained. My cousin's widow recalls:

> *"I remember so clearly the first time your parents visited us, some few months after the war. We went together to visit your mother's sister and your grandmother in Tübingen. It was almost impossible for her to speak German, and only with your father's help could she communicate at all. I was naïve enough to think, 'OK, she hasn't been speaking German for a long time.' But later I realised that there was a deep trauma which just didn't allow her to speak German."*

My mother had not, of course, forgotten her fluency in German. Throughout the war years our home was filled with relatives and friends who had come to England as refugees. Many were elderly and never became fluent in English, so it was natural for my parents to converse with them in their mother tongue. I can well understand that the shock of her return to Germany after all that had happened was difficult and distressing for my mother. She would have had a natural wish to emphasise her strong identification with her new homeland, and to highlight her feeling of alienation from the country of her birth, and a subconscious way of achieving this might have been through her demonstration of an obvious dependence on the use of the English language.

This perception was reflected in a BBCTV 'Timewatch' programme, *Children of the Third Reich*, broadcast in the autumn of 1993. It describes a meeting that took place in April 1993 between five people whose fathers had been high ranking Nazi officials, convicted Nazi criminals, and ten whose parents or grandparents had been killed in the concentration camps or ghettoes of Nazi occupied Europe. Everyone involved was deeply apprehensive. During the five days they were together, initial inhibition turned to increasingly honest and open discussion. A waterfall of emotion was released. The effect was cathartic. The children of the Nazi criminals witnessed the pain of the irretrievable loss suffered by their Jewish companions. They in their turn began to understand the crushing weight of guilt carried by their companions and realised that their lives, and probably the lives of their children also, had been totally destroyed. This understanding led to a reconciliation that could perhaps only have been achieved in the unique atmosphere of Neve Shalom/ Wahat al Salam, (Oasis of Peace) the Israeli peace village. One of the Jewish women summed up her feelings at the end:

> *"What I had feared more than anything else was that these people would find some way of explaining away what happened during the Holocaust, or that they would rationalize what their fathers did. I knew I would not be able to tolerate that. When I saw how devastated their lives were as a result of having the fathers they had I saw that we were two sides of one coin."*

Nevertheless, the question does remain as to how the German nation, once widely regarded as amongst the most sophisticated and cultured in Europe, could so quickly be corrupted and debased as to show widespread support, even enthusiasm, for one of the most brutal and depraved regimes in human history. Dorothy Macardle, journalist and psychologist, carried out a detailed study of the affect the terrible wartime experience had on the *Children of Europe* which was published in 1949 in a book of that name. The first chapter, entitled *To Create a Nazi*, provides insight into how the Nazi regime was able to achieve such a total distortion of a nation's soul. She writes:

> *Germans who were children in the late twenties and thirties were destined to an odious fate and to world execration, yet most of them had years of great happiness - of hope and idealism and pride - when they believed themselves to be the most fortunate generation ever born. One could not meet them in their youth groups anywhere without being struck by their air of vitality. Singing as they marched, they radiated a sense of health and purpose in a disorientated age. There*

71

was nothing in their demeanour to suggest that they were in training for such tasks as are typified by names like Belsen and Lidice, yet such was the destiny towards which they marched.

These were Hitler's first victims - the children of Germany. Fired to a white heat of devotion, they were hammered and twisted, like iron on the anvil, into weapons for his ends. Such a calculated distortion of human minds is not recorded elsewhere in history; and, in fact, it could not have taken place at any much earlier date, since the psychological knowledge and the resources for mass suggestion by means of which it was accomplished were comparatively new.

The Nazi leaders were supreme opportunists; their place and time offered them an extraordinary combination of elements helpful to their purpose...Fanatics need a common cause and a common enemy. Hitler found both at hand. Opposition to Communism provided the cause, all the more satisfying because Communism had its centre and source among the Slav peoples whom Germans had long been taught to despise. Russia provided a remote object for hate; and there was another at home - a minority, 'alien' in origin, composed of people who were formidable rivals in commerce, too gifted, too poor or too wealthy to be easily accommodated - the Jews.

The hour invited the man, and the man possessed a curious intuitive knowledge of his own people - knew, in his own words, how to "inspire the masses and drive them forward in a sort of hysterical trance."

Seeing in retrospect the terrible descent down which young Germans were being drawn, it is difficult to realise that they were inspired by what was, in the beginning, no ignoble appeal. ...For a time membership of

the Hitler Youth movement was voluntary and the
attractions were those natural to youth. The baser
appeals came later, when the sensitiveness of boyhood
had been blunted and when the Nazi system had closed
on German youth like a trap.   *(16)*

The Hitler Youth Movement was started long before Hitler came to power, in the mid 1920s. It was, from the first, detested by liberals, and by some clergymen and teachers and parents. For a time it was banned in some states, but it grew prolifically nevertheless, absorbing one after another of the young people's clubs and organisations. In 1926 it was named *Hitler Jugend*, and an organisation for girls, *Bund Deutscher Maedel*, was formed in 1928. When Baldur von Schirach was promoted in 1932 to head Hitler Youth he had 35,000 young people under his charge. He, himself a product of the movement, was only 23 years old at the time.   According to Stephen Roberts, (one-time Professor of Modern History at the University of Sydney) by 1935 there were Hitler Youth groups in 53 countries as well as in Germany, and its membership numbered six million. As the children in Germany grew older they were forced to spend more and more time devoted to Hitler Youth activities at the expense of school education; and the activities being developed were not those of a normal school curriculum, but marching and street fighting, book burning and, above all, Jew baiting and the vandalism of Jewish property. Without them the fate of Hitler's other victims might have been very different.   Dorothy Macardle in no way suggests that under the Nazi regime the behaviour of many 'ordinary' German people was anything other than absolutely abhorrent, but she does provide some explanation as to how so many could so quickly, so effectively, so ruthlessly have been corrupted.

All of us in our small group of witnesses would have been of an age to be involved in these activities. For Paul, his exclusion from membership of Hitler Youth was one of many causes of his increasing sense of isolation. He remembers feeling left out - of missing the cameraderie of belonging to a group of friends.

"I was only six and had had just 3 months at school
when, in 1938, we were forced to flee to Berlin. But

73

*even in that short time I couldn't understand why I was
so isolated. I didn't suffer any harassment at school,
but I couldn't play with other children - or rather - they
couldn't play with me. And they all had smart little
Hitler Jugend uniforms and I didn't and so I began to
feel different. I wasn't persecuted by the other children
for being a Jewish child, but became very aware that
somehow I was different. So I became very attached to
home - more attached than a child should be - clinging
as it were."*

We can only echo the words of Paul's father when he thanked God for
the grace bestowed on him by having been born a Jew *"...for who knows
what otherwise I might have done."*

True reconciliation can come about only if the past has been honestly
confronted, so it was my intention to ask my witnesses when had they
first found out the terrible truth about the Holocaust, and what had their
reaction been? But I found that these were questions I could not ask.
Only with Eve could I discuss this in depth, because our conversation
had already begun long ago on our journey in India. Eve told me that:

*"I realised that my parents were likely to have been caught
up in these terrible events. I suppose in a way it was a
relief to hear for certain about my parents' and brother's
fate. It was devastating news, but I think I knew anyway.
There was never a moment when I could say, 'My parents
have died. They have been killed.' It was a gradual realisation."*

Eve returned to Prague in 1965 to visit her only surviving uncle and aunt:

*"They gave me a sort of background and helped to fill in
the picture of my family. Once they started to tell me what
had happened to them all, I felt that I had had it very easy,
and I felt guilty because of that. Survivors do feel guilty.
Why did I survive and not my brother? The first
opportunity I had to grieve for my family was when my*

aunt took me to the Memorial Synagogue. The walls were completely covered with the names of all the Czech Jews who had perished in the camps. To go along the walls till one got to the letter P, and then to find one's father's name, one's mother's name, one's brother's name, and uncles and cousins. That really hit you then, because they were there, in front of your eyes. Thousands and thousands and thousands of others. And that was when I really did let go and burst into tears and I cried and cried and couldn't stop. In a way that sort of exorcises the pain. I hadn't ever had a moment when somebody could say, 'Your parents died yesterday,' so that I could weep then, and mourn properly."

Eve's testimony is a moving statement for all those in our group whose sense of loss will never ease. I could not ask others to go through the pain of recalling the shock of their first realisation of the terrible fate of their relatives and friends.

When the full horror of the atrocities committed in the concentration camps was revealed after the war I also found it too difficult to cope with the truth. I simply did not want to know. It made my shame at having been born a German even harder to bear. In 1989 I visited Yad Vashem. It was a pilgrimage which I had to make for the sake of my grandparents. Eve has also found it difficult to cope with the whole terrible truth, and with far more reason than I:

"It was very difficult to face the reality. It is a good thing that there was no television at that time, though there were word pictures on the radio and in the newspapers. I suppose there were photographs, but I don't remember actually seeing pictures of what was found in the concentration camps. Perhaps my English Mum hid them from me. I realised that my parents and brother were likely to have been caught up in these terrible events about which I heard and read from news reports."

As one gradually comes to accept the inescapable truths of the past it also becomes easier to disassociate oneself from the burden of guilt. *Schindler's List* was the first film about the Holocaust I had ever seen. I have never had the courage to watch another. Eve has a letter about her parents' death. She has read it once. It is in her safe keeping, but she cannot read it again. One might think that with time the pain would ease. It is clear that it does not. As we grow older there is more time to reflect. Memories of the past grow more vivid. Our childhood experience matters more, not less. Dorit Bader Whiteman found, as I did, that those she interviewed are more emotionally affected now than they have ever been:

> *"They say they are more stirred by the events as time goes by...the limited years ahead seem to focus the glance backward. The value of life seems enhanced and losses are recognised more clearly."* (17)

The realisation that some members of our group might not be able to talk about the fate of their parents was almost instinctive. I sensed that this sorrow could only be shared if my witnesses chose to reveal these memories themselves. One could not ask them to do so. The deeply repressed feelings from which many children of the victims of Nazi murder suffer are explained by Bruno Bettelheim in his essay *Children of the Holocaust*. He writes:

> *"There are a number of reasons why they cannot talk about it, do not wish to talk about it. It is not that they want to avoid thinking about what happened, because they have never for a moment been able to forget it; they have been obsessed by it all their lives. They are convinced that no words are adequate to express what happened; no words can put it to rest. ...Those who listen may think they understand ...but at best they can comprehend only the facts, having no real comprehension of the nature of the suffering. What good would it then do to speak about it?*
>
> *In order to be able to construct for themselves a modus vivendi, they hid their true feeling so deeply...that they can*

hardly reach it themselves. They did this in order to be able to continue to live; to do well at school, to pass exams, to prepare for a profession, and later to marry, to have children, to try to meet the obligations of family life.

The tragedy is that fate has prevented them from grieving for their parents, from mourning for them, and that is why their old wounds cannot heal. Even under normal circumstances it is difficult to give up hoping for the return of a parent who has suddenly disappeared without trace - especially for a child - the wish to believe that the missing person is still alive is so strong that some proof is needed before the unhappy fact will be accepted. This holds true even in normal circumstances, and the conditions in which these children lived were far from normal..." *(18)*

Bettelheim makes a very detailed analysis of the complicated psychological reactions of *Children of the Holocaust* and the long term effects of their experience. The insights he offers are certainly relevant to most members of our group. Here is revealed the underlying feelings that prevented Eve from truly mourning the death of her parents and her brother until she saw their names inscribed upon the walls of Prague's Memorial Synagogue. And so it was that with Ruth and Frank I felt the silence and an unexpressed tangible sadness.

The relationship with Germany is difficult, but for most of our group reconciliation has come with time, and with a younger generation of Germans. But it has not come easily. Apart from Paul and Kurt, only Ruth and Luke have returned to Germany for any length of time. Ruth found great difficulty in coming to terms with her German background, but her emotions were very complicated. She was trying not only to find reconciliation with Germany, but also to rebuild a relationship with her parents, and this, sadly, was never achieved:

"When I first went back I rejected Germany just as Germany had rejected me. Now I can thoroughly enjoy visiting my brother, who did eventually go back to live there. But he wasn't forced to go back (as Ruth had

been) *so he had time for reconciliation, and now he is*
very rooted there. But I still feel very ambivalent about
Germany. There is a part of me that can't deny my
German roots. There are certain things about the
culture, the music, some of the literature, even some of
the cooking, that I do identify with. But at a safe dis-
tance!"

Luke never sensed any anti-German feeling in his home, although his
father rarely went back, but he did feel increasingly uncomfortable about
being German in the aftermath of the war. He decided to form his own
impressions, so in 1961 he worked in Germany for six months. He said,
"What was interesting was that I felt incredibly at home in Germany and
I feel very at home speaking German." Luke's experience appears to be
atypical of our group. Perhaps the nature of his work, and the company
of other young dedicated doctors placed Germany's rejection of his family
far away from his immediate experience. The reconciliatory influence
of his father also had probably been crucial to Luke's positive attitude.

My own attitude to Germany was also strongly influenced by my father.
After the war, desperate for news of his parents, he turned to the parents
of my friend Emma for help and advice. Through their contact with
Quakers they were able to put him in touch with members of the Friends
Ambulance Units who were working in Germany - pursuing their traditional role of bringing relief to the destitute, hope to the demoralised
people, building bridges of understanding across which reconciliation
could be reached. As soon as he could get the necessary permits, and
with help from the FAU, my father went to his parents' home-town of
Bielefeld. FAU officials who were involved in tracing missing people
and reuniting families, were soon able to establish the sad circumstances
of his parents' death; and not only of theirs but that of many of his aunts
and uncles, cousins and friends, most of whom perished in August 1942
either in, or on their way to Auschwitz. That it was Quakers, with their
long experience of all aspects of the work of reconciliation, who broke
this news to him was, I believe, absolutely crucial to his ability to come
to terms with his loss. They understood his pain and what his long term
reaction to this personal tragedy might be; but he had his own inner
strengths too. Anticipating the anguish and guilt my non-Jewish mother

would feel, he followed the advice given to him by the FAU to cross the ravaged war-torn country of his youth to visit my grandmother and my aunts in Tübingen before coming home to share his grief with her. To her dying day my grandmother talked about the warmth of that first reunion after the war, and of the comfort which that emotional reconciliation had given her. I never once heard my father express any hatred of Germans or of Germany, nor for that matter of any other nation or group of people. His ability to relate to all people in all walks of life has been an inspiration which I try to emulate, but could never hope to achieve. Because of him I feel at ease in Germany, although it has taken me a lifetime to shed my shame at having been born there.

Eva, like me, has lied about her birthplace! Unlike her I cannot escape my shame by claiming a Jewish connection which I do not feel. She says:

> "I was always proud to be Jewish, but anything German was anathema - anything German, the language - anything! Even now it's at the back of my mind. If someone asks me whether I am German I deny it and reply that I am Jewish first. When we go abroad and people comment on how well I speak German I always lie and say that I lived there for a few years before the war. I cannot say that I was born in Germany. I would rather people didn't know. For me it is something shaming."

Kurt had to go back to Germany in 1950 to manage his father's factory when it was returned under the German government programme of restitution. He hoped to sell it and return to England within six months, but it was not that simple and he had to stay for four difficult years:

> "I feel very uncomfortable whenever I am in Germany. I always get out as quickly as I can. I sometimes go to Werther to visit friends, go to the cemetery and walk in the countryside. But I know that there are groups of the extreme right again. When I was there in 1950 we used to travel to buy tobacco, staying in small hotels or inns. I didn't want to meet people so I used to go up to my room.

You just don't know who you are sitting next to and you can't help wondering what he did in the war. But I used to hear the locals singing the old beer songs, and I would wake up sweating at the memories."

For Ida, Frank and Eve, whose parents were killed in concentration camps, reconciliation is far more difficult. Eve has found it impossible during most of her adult life even to talk to German people, let alone to visit Germany. She told me:

"I didn't want to have anything to do with Germans or with Germany. As soon as I knew someone was German that was it! I just didn't want to find out anything more. A shutter came down. I froze. I was fifty before I could feel easy in the company of Germans and talk to them. My husband and I went to visit his friend in Germany, and his wife and children. They were lovely! The friend's father was there too. I just couldn't talk to him. I had this feeling as soon as I met him that, although he was charming and polite, he was of an age to have been in some position of authority in the war. But that visit was a watershed, because I realised that you can't visit the sins of one generation upon their children."

Ida speaks with equal passion:

"I am not particularly pleased to meet Germans and to discuss their past or my past or their future with them. I just feel so resentful and so saddened by my parents' fate that I can't be unemotional. And when I'm told, as I was recently, that, 'Really we don't mind Jews very much these days!' that is like a red rag to a bull! I replied, 'Because of your anti-Semitic attitudes you have lost many scientists, many musicians and many authors and you are the poorer for it.' So I am not a particularly generous spirit when it comes to my relationship with Germany."

80

Frank agreed and emphasised the importance of not allowing a younger generation to be in ignorance of those times. He believes that in recent times the whole horror of the Holocaust has been allowed to disappear from the German school curriculum. *"In their own interest these things should never be forgotten."* But on this Paul seems to disagree with Frank's opinion. He is more concerned about the rise of right wing extremism in England and France than in Germany.

> *"There are more people who have learned from German history and who know the consequences of right wing extremism in Germany. Resistance to it is greater in Germany than here. Among my young German friends many still have a feeling of shame at being German. I tell them not to be ashamed. I tell them that I lost my grandmother in the Holocaust, but they didn't kill her. Neo-fascism is at least as bad in England as it is in Germany. Why should they feel guilty? I tell them to accept their identity."*

However, like all of us, Paul himself went through a period of deep resentment. This caused him to stay for only one year of the two-year study-fellowship he had been awarded at Bonn University. He was shocked at the shallowness of the post war 'Get Rich Quick' materialism which seemed to characterise German society at that time. He had to work through these negative feelings to learn to accept Germans as human beings of equal worth. His ties with Germany were to become very strong, and not only because his wife was born there. From 1956 until the fall of the communist regimes in 1989, he was the East European adviser to the British Council of Churches. The core of this ministry was in East Germany which he visited many times. The courage of many of those with whom he worked in standing up to this other dictatorship, rekindled his respect for many German people. He will not have been surprised at the emotional response of young Germans to the film *Schindler's List*.

It is only to be expected that those of us who left Germany early, Renate, Luke and I, and therefore escaped the direct experience of persecution and terror suffered by others in our group, should find an easier relationship with Germany. Bearing in mind the irretrievable losses suffered by other members of the group, it is impressive that they all achieved a reconciliation deep enough to accept a friendly relationship with the postwar generation of Germans.

RECONCILIATION - ISRAEL

There is also a feeling of having a special relationship with Israel, which was reflected in the fact that, without any prompting from me, nearly everyone brought Israel into the conversation. Some of us have relatives out there, and have visited Israel. There is understanding for the precarious existence of this small nation state, and sympathy for the fear and tension which darken everyday life for many Israelis. Nevertheless most of our group expressed uneasy disappointment with the aggressive attitude shown in public and political life. Typical of our reaction are Eva's comments:

> *"I am absolutely ashamed of what they are doing politically, but I can understand them. I mean, if anybody has got a psychological excuse to be absolutely beastly to everybody else, it is Israel, because of the way Jews have been treated. If that is how they have been taught that the world goes round, then that is the rule to follow. But some of the things they have done to their Arab population are appalling - terrible. I am horrified, absolutely horrified about what they have done. It is just like a child who is very difficult and awkward because people have been very cruel. Now there seems to be some hope, but we will have to wait and see."*

Ida also spoke of her unease at Israel's aggressive and chauvinistic stance. She contrasts the philosophy of Judaism, with its emphasis on community responsibility and the creation of a peaceful society, with the reputation Israel has for violent confrontation, and policies which put Israeli Jewish rights above those of other Israeli citizens. She said:

82

*"I don't think it is a very happy state. I cannot identify
with the triumphalist pride in military victories which
they have shown in the past. My parents always emphasised the peaceful ethic of Judaism. They died so quietly
accepting their fate. I cannot rejoice in great feats of
aggression. I don't feel very comfortable when I go
there."*

But Israel breeds doves as well as hawks. Members of our group identify strongly with the very active and courageous Israeli peace movement. Nowhere is the commitment to harmonious co-existence more
inspirationally realised than in Neve Shalom/Wahat al Salam. Here Arab
and Jewish families live together, work together, learn together, celebrate together, pray together; each in their own religious and cultural
tradition; each enriched by the values and beliefs of the other. It is here
that Wellesley Aron, Zionist and teacher, chose to establish his long-held
dream of a School for Peace. Like us, Wellesley had been exposed to
hostile harassment. Born in London in 1901 of German-Jewish parents,
he grew up in a typical English upper-middle class environment. In
1914, shortly before the outbreak of the First World War, he was suddenly removed from his public school and taken to Germany to live with
his mother's family. Here he was humiliated by the hostile anti-British
sentiments expressed, not only by German society at large, but also by
the family themselves. This was one of many experiences which set
him on a lifelong pilgrimage in search of peace and reconciliation. He
found in Neve Shalom/Wahat al Salam the perfect environment for his
School for Peace. It is also perhaps the only place where the children
of Holocaust victims and the children of convicted Nazi war criminals
could have built the bridges of understanding which enabled them to
reach each other.

PACIFISM

Bearing in mind the deep discomfort which members of our group feel
about the aggressive character of the Israeli regime, it is not surprising
that there is a strong conviction that much could be achieved by a greater
emphasis on reconciliation and mediation, but on pacifism as a political

reality there is divided opinion. The only totally committed pacifist is Paul. He says:

> *"I am a very convinced pacifist. If I am challenged about what I would have done about Nazi oppression, then I hope that I would have had the courage to stick to my principles as a better way to defeat evil, even Hitler. The degree of mass murder that was faced by the Jews, who were not defended by anyone, that degree of evil is hardly conceivable in peace time. But I believe that evil systems like that can be defeated by non-violent resistance, with less evil done in the process than happened in the war. The war became butchery. There was mass retaliation against German cities, which should not be morally acceptable to us now. The Allies could have stopped Auschwitz. They could have bombed the railways which ran to Auschwitz, but they never tried. They knew very well what was going on and they were asked by International Jewish organizations to do that, but for the Allies this was not a war priority. Killing Germans was important. Saving the lives of Jews wasn't."*

It would be interesting to continue this conversation, to discover what Paul's reaction would be to present-day events in former Yugoslavia. Would he support the bombing of military installations in defence of the civilian population, as has been threatened by NATO in support of UN resolutions? Eve picks up this dilemma:

> *"To begin with, my childhood experiences made me very pacifist. I just hated the thought of war. I think that on the whole I am still a pacifist, but the idea is not easy, and events like the civil war in Bosnia and now in Kosovo make one think. This has made me question the whole concept of nationalism, and racism, and all the related issues about which people go to war. What really depressed me was to get back to post-revolutionary Czechoslovakia and to find prejudice and racism much worse than here, and strong nationalism as well. They are very prejudiced*

against all minorities, such as gypsies, Hungarians, and Jews - still! People just don't seem to learn anything from their experiences."

The discussions about pacifism always turned (as was only to be expected in the context of the interviews) on the issue of how the Nazi regime could have been defeated. All of us in our group would like to be able to agree with Paul, but cannot see any alternative to the use of force in defence of the defenceless. Renate said:

"The issue of pacifism is very difficult. When one sees all the horrors of war one is bound to feel pacifist, as an ideal. But if opponents know that you are not going to fight back or resist, what are they likely to do? If the British hadn't fought back when the Germans were aiming to dominate the whole of Europe they would have spread their anti-Semitism, and their brutal philosophy might have destroyed civilization as we know it."

Ida emphasised the importance of a democratic tradition to the success or otherwise of passive resistance. In the Germany she had known there was no tradition of freely expressed disagreement and therefore no experience of organised opposition:

"There was very little expression of individual ideas or opposition in Germany, very little real democracy, which we take so much for granted in Britain. They could not have organised a peaceful resistance. People were so easily led, so easily influenced. So, what could the Jews do in the face of all that power and might? Quite honestly, they would have been gunned down immediately."

Frank takes up her point. The landlady with whom he had lodged as a young student in Birmingham was a Quaker. She had argued cogently with him about her pacifist convictions, and believed that Hitler could have been defeated by the sheer moral force of people who opposed him. But Frank questions her conviction:

"But, would it have happened in one's own lifetime? Is this a defensible stance? To say that one is prepared to give up one's freedom - one's life possibly - in the hope that sometime in the future the forces of good would overcome the forces of evil? No! I am very glad that we had Churchill in this country to fight Hitler. When we try to visualise what the world would have been like, and it would probably have remained under Hitler for a very long time - at least one generation - we are forced to balance the evil of war against this absolutely unimaginable evil."

RACE RELATIONS IN BRITAIN

While everyone in our group harbours unease and some disaffection in their relationship with Germany, and with Israel, we would all claim that our sensitivity to racist attitudes and to discrimination against minority groups has been heightened by our own experience. This may not seem entirely logical; but it is possible that in these particular relationships our attitudes are overwhelmed by personal emotions, so that we tend to stereotype those we identify as aggressors. Racism Awareness Training, which first alerted me to the nature of my own self-prejudice, and which is often used to nurture anti-racist attitudes in those engaged in public services, (for example teachers and social workers) can never equal in its intensity what one learns from bitter experience. So it is not surprising that in our group we feel we have special empathy for those who are unjustly exposed to harassment, persecution and discrimination in their daily lives, such as the Palestinian citizens of Israel. Racist attitudes are, sadly, endemic to us all, as Ruth explains:

"It is deeply part of the human mental make up to define ourselves by identifying 'the other'. We see ourselves as part of a group and we then say, 'We belong to this group. So we are not one of them.' In times of difficulty 'the other' is blamed and becomes a scapegoat. That underlies the whole question of difference and race, which is not something that exists, because scientifically you can

prove that there is no such thing as race. Self esteem comes into this as well, because 'We' are always better than 'They' are. When there is stress then racism will flare up. I don't know that it has got worse. It is always there, but in times of peace and plenty you get nearer to harmony."

Hence the crucial nature of our childhood search for self-identity in our new homeland. Affirmation of a child's racial, cultural and faith background is an important aspect of education for Britain's multiracial society. It is now regarded as essential in building a child's self-esteem, but was singularly unrecognised when most of us were at school. The affirmation of a child's sense of self-worth formed the core of the changes introduced into the school curriculum during the 1980s. Anti-racist multicultural teaching was highlighted by being given status as a National Priority Area, thus attracting generous government funding for In Service Training of teachers. Now, just at a time when race relations in Britain are very strained, this important aspect of education has been marginalised by other concerns.

The state of race relations in Britain was brought into the discussion by everyone in our group. We all feel that racism is on the increase, and that many minority groups have reason to live in fear. Luke comes into daily contact with patients who are suffering directly from the tension and stress of life in the multi-racial community of Kennington. He feels that there is a lot more racial tension than people are prepared to admit:

"I think the situation is rather depressing. In the past I had a feeling that Britain had a way of life which coped well with racial disharmony. Some of this feeling goes back to the way in which the English temperament seemed to cope with the disasters which were about to befall the country at the outbreak of the war. Everyone here was quietly clipping their hedges and getting on with life in a calm way, whereas in Germany everyone would be sitting in the local café tearing their hair out about the likely dangers. Now I am much less confident that the British

character and the British temperament can cope with the problems which face us. I don't think that the average Englishman is terribly aware of what is happening around him. What was seen as a great quality at one time is now beginning to appear to me as really dangerous ignorance about how the community functions and about its sense of values. I asked a friend of mine who works at the Department of Applied Linguistics in Edinburgh University what the British students have in common with the continental students who come to study in his department. He told me that there is very little contact between them and that it is very striking how different their conversations are. The British students talk mostly about sport and sex! A group of students from almost any other country - say France or Greece, Poland or Germany - within a very short time are talking about politics; not party politics, but about the politics of Life. There seems to be a real lack of meaningful debate about the issues that really matter, about our values and about the development of our life as a community.

Others in the group would agree with Luke. Renate and Eva, talked of economic deterioration as a root cause of mounting racial tension. The search for scapegoats, the 'them' which Ruth talked about, is the result. Paul identified political extremism as an additional factor:

"The Tory Party conference of October 1993 came mighty close to being a fascist assembly in mood, so I am worried. People at the bottom of the economic pile, who feel very insecure, believe that foreigners have taken away their homes and their jobs. They are encouraged (in this belief) *by sophisticated intellectuals; politicians who want their votes and therefore start talking their language. In Germany it was the Jews who were blamed, who were the scapegoats; now it is the Turks. And in London it is the Pakistanis. And everywhere there is residual anti-Semitism."*

88

This is an analysis with which all of our group would identify. Or are we super-sensitive in our own way of interpreting the mood of society around us? Eve developed this theme on a broader canvas:

"There seems to be an increase in the need to belong to a group, to identify with a group. You see this in religious fundamentalism. It is a palliative for an underlying unease. If you are insecure you need to latch onto something. It can be nationalism or religion. It is a kind of toe hold and if you feel yourself falling, as things around you disintegrate, you have something to cling to. The nicest, most valuable people are those who don't feel loyalty just to one country or one group, like Yehudi Menuhin or Peter Ustinov, who seem to belong everywhere and anywhere. If you asked me what nationality they are I wouldn't know, and for them it obviously doesn't matter. They belong to the Human Race."

The heightened sensitivity to racism, or any form of negative discrimination is, we feel, a positive effect of our experience. Eva said:

"I am certainly more aware of unfair discrimination of any kind than I might have been. I get very upset and angry when I come across it. Also, due to my problem of depression, which has happened pretty regularly since I suffered the trauma in Germany, I am much more in sympathy with people who have mental trouble, often due to something that has happened to them during their lives. Possibly I might have just ignored them, or told them to 'pull themselves together.' But my troubles have helped me to understand."

CLOUDED LIVES

Numbered among those with mental problems which developed from their experience of life are some who came to Britain on the Kindertransports. Both Barry Turner and Dorit Bader Whiteman write movingly about children who were overwhelmed by their ordeal. Not everyone could cope with the pain of their uprooting. Torn from their parents, their home, their friends, their language, their whole world seemed to have fallen apart. All that they loved, all that they had known had vanished. Many were far too young to understand what was happening to them or the reason for the traumatic change. To be told then, as many were, that they 'should be grateful,' was asking too much. For the most part everyone involved was totally dedicated to the welfare of the children who had been rescued. Under the very difficult conditions of wartime Britain, everyone concerned was doing their best. Ruth has dedicated much of her work as a psychotherapist to helping some of those from whom the cloud of despair has never lifted. She doubts whether any statistics exist about the number of *Kinder* who have needed psychiatric care, partly because of a patient's right of confidentiality. In addition, she suggests that it would be difficult to define with sufficient accuracy who should be included in this specific category. Records which might have given some indication about the number of children who broke down under the strain have been destroyed, or are confidential. But of the need for special help there is no doubt. Ruth says:

"Those who ask for and are able to use psychotherapy are not the real 'casualty group' because they are able to experience their need for help, ask for it and use it. The real 'casualties' either do not admit they need help or are unable to ask for it. Some are unable to benefit even when help is offered. This is very distressing for all concerned, and is perhaps a repeat of the original distress of their trauma."

While we must never underestimate the distress which destroyed the lives of some of the child refugees, what should astonish us is not that some have suffered, but that most of the children were able to cope so well, and recovered from their ordeal even strengthened, perhaps, by the challenges they had to face. It is interesting to speculate on why this crucial difference exists, between those who could cope with the trauma of their uprooting, and those who were destroyed by it. The work of those like Ruth, who are committed to helping the casualties, will perhaps generate greater expertise and understanding, which will be of benefit to future child refugees who face similar problems in coming to terms with life in their new homeland.

LIFE COMMITMENTS

The pain lies on the dark side of the cloud that hangs over mankind as a legacy of the Hitler regime. But there are some positives behind the negative. One has already been identified - a heightened awareness of racism or discrimination. Dorit Bader Whiteman identifies an unusual determination to succeed as another. She believes that this comes from a feeling - subconscious perhaps - that we owe a debt of gratitude and therefore have an obligation to make something of our lives:

> *"The desire, or perhaps the acute need in this group to render services to mankind is extraordinarily high. I would venture a guess that it is the dedication to human causes that is a factor in alleviating any guilt* (about their survival) *they might otherwise feel. They filled the pages* (of her research questionnaire) *not only with descriptions of what they do but also with explanations of why they do it."*   *(19)*

That analysis I believe holds true for each person in our group. We will never know where life might have taken us if circumstances had been different, but we do recognise that out of a negative some positive can come. And the need to *'render services to mankind'* does appear to manifest itself in what we have chosen to do with our lives. In our group there happen to be five teachers; Ida, Renate, Eve, Ruth and me. In addition Frank and Luke are involved in teaching at university level. It is pure chance that so many of those who agreed to take part in this project happen to have chosen teaching as a career, and each of us has developed a special role which makes us feel that it has been a worthwhile and rewarding profession. Ida's attitude to her pupils has been influenced by her experience:

> *"I shall always be specially sympathetic to people who are disadvantaged. My own experiences have given me*

91

*a deeper insight into people's way of thinking, so the coun-
selling and caring aspect of being a personal tutor is as
near to the caring role of a doctor (which is what I had
originally planned to be) as I could hope to get."*

Ruth has also used her negative childhood experiences in a positive way.
Like Ida, she found the counselling and pastoral care of her students particularly rewarding, and this led her eventually to a career as a psychotherapist. The help she is now able to give to Holocaust survivors,
to Jewish refugees and to their children, draws on her own experiences:

> *"The upheavals and traumas of my childhood, my own
> experience of feeling rejected, of losing my roots, of inse-
> curity, have given me a greater awareness of how others
> feel."*

Renate found a special role in the Schools Inspectorate, which enabled
her to influence other teachers through In Service Training. She could
pass on her belief that:

> *"As a teacher one has to adjust to all the different per-
> sonalities that make children the way they are. It is respect
> for the individual and all good teachers must have that
> respect. I have learned how necessary it is to be tolerant
> of differences and to seek out and foster the positive and
> unique contribution that each person can make."*

Eve, also, found the pastoral care of pupils to be a most rewarding aspect
of teaching. When she retired, her wish to continue to be of service
found expression through voluntary work:

> *"I decided to help adult immigrants and taught English
> to a young Pakistani woman. This was more than just
> teaching really, it was befriending and helping her and
> her family to settle here. That was a direct response to
> knowing what it feels like to be a stranger and a for-
> eigner in a country. My involvement as an Oxfam vol-
> unteer stems from my own experience as well."*

It was through our work for Oxfam that Eve and I met. Eve expresses eloquently the reasons for our commitment:

> *"It is not so much the famine relief which makes this work important to us. It is the fight against injustice, the fight on behalf of the underprivileged. It is the political aspects of Oxfam's work which are important to us, helping the poorest to gain their rights."*

Both of us recognise that our own experience of having been 'outsiders' has informed our attitudes, and we value the opportunity Oxfam gives us to make a contribution to help others who are 'outsiders' because they are marginalised by their poverty. The experience I gained as an Education Volunteer for Oxfam led directly to my appointment by the West Sussex Education Department as co-ordinator for Multicultural Education and the relevant In Service Training necessary to support teachers. This gave me the opportunity to work with them in the classroom on projects to enhance racial harmony. The aim was to build bridges of understanding between the children who come from the many different racial and cultural groups which make up the rich tapestry of Britain today.

Ida can speak for all of us who are committed to teaching, including Luke and Frank, when she says:

> *"Life is a long pilgrimage of learning. Jews have by tradition a great respect for learning and this has helped them through many difficulties. I feel that my father instilled into me a great respect for learning, and I think that I have lived by his philosophy that knowledge is the most valuable gift you can have."*

Having lost so much herself, she could add that education is also a gift which no one can take away.

Eva devoted her life to music and derived great satisfaction from passing on her enthusiasm to a younger generation by her work as a teacher and Youth Orchestra tutor. This brought her into contact with children from a variety of cultural backgrounds. *"What a way to earn a living! Very*

hard work, certainly! But sheer pleasure and immensely satisfying."
She makes light of her dedication, but Eva gave total commitment to her responsibilities both as an orchestral player, and as a teacher, which enabled her to make a valuable contribution to the development of the talent and enthusiasm of many a young musician.

Paul recognises in every aspect of his multi-faceted career as political activist and church leader, the influence of earlier experiences. He felt this connection particularly strongly when he was Chairman of the British Section of Amnesty International. His commitment to this very responsible role he traces directly to the influence of his maternal grandfather, who became the village policeman, and diligently worked his way up until in the early 1930s he was appointed Deputy Governor of the prison in the town where Paul was born. Paul remembers playing with the prisoners in the prison yard, and as a result he has never had any fear of prisons or of prisoners. But Hitler's policy of silencing his opponents was about to change the life of this Deputy Governor of the prison in Thüringen:

> *"In 1937 the first political prisoners of the Nazi era were brought to the prison. They were communists. My grandfather was an old fashioned 'Beampte' (bureaucrat), conservative, right wing, but upright with very strong principles. He disagreed completely with the politics of communism, but he was furious that these people, who had not been accused of any crime, who were not criminals, should be imprisoned. And so he resigned. He put his keys on the governor's desk and said, 'I have not been appointed to keep people in prison who are not criminals.' That has influenced my life probably more than any other single event. I would never have become Chairman of Amnesty International later in my life if it hadn't been for this powerful formative experience so early in my life."*

Paul's influence has been profoundly important to many people in all walks of life. Until recently he was Director of International Ministry at Coventry Cathedral where he had great opportunity to give outstanding service and he continues to be actively involved in promoting the causes of international peace and justice.

Kurt and his wife Charlotte have devoted the last thirty years of their lives to the welfare of foreign students through their commitment to the creation of Nansen Village in North London. This stems directly from their own experience of growing up in an alien environment, and also from a strong feeling that through this work they could repay the 'debt of gratitude' they feel they owe to all the people who helped them in their early years as refugees. They identified as a specially relevant problem the difficulty many foreign students have in finding decent affordable accommodation in London. Postgraduate students, sometimes married and with small children, seemed to face the greatest obstacles, and often encountered overtly hostile racial attitudes. The answer was to provide purpose-built housing. Kurt and Charlotte invested both time and money into this venture, and they have been totally committed to it since the first stages of planning. They were helped with government grants and donations from friends and supporters of the scheme. Now, in the beautiful grounds of two dilapidated and over-large Victorian mansions, since demolished, stands Nansen Village. It is named after the Nobel Peace Prize-winning Norwegian explorer, scientist, and philanthropist, who himself worked on behalf of refugees. It offers modestly-priced accommodation for 65 students and their families. The present residents come from 30 different countries.

Here they have not just a home, but also security, friendship and mutual support. In the community hall they can meet each other, share ideas, organise social events and give each other encouragement. The Nansen Village nursery school has become quite well known in the area, and now takes children from outside the community as well as the young children of the residents. Some of its success must be attributed to Renate, who is a Trustee, and has been able to give valuable advice. Kurt feels that it is a privilege to have had the opportunity to make a contribution in this way:

"Whether my life work with Nansen Village has anything to do with our experience of Nazi persecution and its effect on our lives, or whether I might have become involved in

Kurt with children of the Nursery Class at Nansen Village

this sort of work anyway I just don't know. Charlotte and I feel we must do something for others who are not as fortunate as we are. We were taken in. We were strangers. We felt we should do something for the country that has been so generous. I feel that the student families who live in Nansen Village will go back to their country taking with them happy memories and a good impression of this country. So we are making a contribution by helping many students from many countries, and at the same time we are helping the country that helped us."

Luke's family have sometimes talked together about their unusual commitment to their professions. This is demonstrated not only in Luke's career, but also those of his brothers and sister. His eldest brother, Michael, is a Professor of Law at the University of London, an expert on legal reform about which he has written and spoken, and whose opinion is widely sought. Angelica is an art historian who has focussed her enthusiasm on developing a more active and lively culture in museums and art galleries both in Britain and overseas. Ben is an inspirational teacher of music, based for the last 25 years at the New England

Conservatoire in Boston. He is also an internationally acclaimed conductor, whose original approach and legendary pre-concert talks make music enjoyably accessible to the audience. His philosophy about leadership and creativity, derived from his work with orchestras, has become a valued source of inspiration to business and professional organisations whom he is frequently asked to address. Luke's particular area of concern, both as a General Practitioner and as a teacher at St Thomas' Hospital, is in medical ethics; people's right to choose their own sort of care, which depends on the relationship between doctor and patient. This has led to an interest in maternity care and home births, and related issues about which there has been considerable conflict between obstetricians and their patients. Luke explains:

"In trying to identify what the effect of the immigration might have been on our development, it is interesting to realise that all four of us children have been actively engaged in trying to change the status quo in our own particular field. We have spent much of our professional life swimming against the conventional tide, which is not always the most comfortable path to follow. One may ask from what early experiences has the drive to follow this road derived? My father, from as long as I can remember, always held in high regard the work ethic, not for its own sake, but from a belief in its importance to human enrichment and satisfaction. My mother possessed to an extraordinary extent the characteristic of never taking 'no' for an answer. Nothing would ever appear impossible to her and the fact that something was not usually done in no way prevented her from doing it!

I am sure that these two very different and exceedingly strong characteristics complemented each other as factors in our upbringing, and gave us all a feeling of confidence in following a path which was often at odds with accepted convention. It is impossible to say to what extent these influences were related to my parents having to emigrate and all the traumas associated with this, but if one refers to the example of other situations where individuals are exposed to challenges of different sorts, the response of those with the necessary resources is frequently stimulated to greater activity and effort."

Everyone in our group has been exposed to challenge and adversity, especially those who have had to build their life in a new homeland, on their own, without parents or family to help and guide them. The courage and determination they needed to succeed and to make a worthwhile contribution was perhaps inherited, in the first place, from their parents. But, in Luke's words, it was the challenging nature of their circumstances which *"stimulated a greater activity and effort."*

Several of our group have identified also a certain strength of character which they believe developed because they were forced to face the harsh reality of life at an early age. Dorit Bader Whiteman wrote of those she interviewed:

> *"They judge their experience to have been character building ... of necessity they were forced to develop or strengthen qualities that later stood them in good stead, the ability to face crises and withstand stress, greater self confidence ... the extra demands made on them in their youth imparted some unique qualities not possessed by other people ... a worldly wisdom that they might not otherwise have acquired."*   (20)

Eva believes that she is a more caring person than she might have been and comments, *"It certainly made me mature very fast!"* Even as an eleven year old she had felt a need to respond in a quite adult way to the anxiety she saw so clearly expressed by her mother. On the morning after Kristallnacht she recalls:

> *"I'd never been so frightened in my life before. I remember sitting there, praying, thinking - What's going to happen? Whatever I do I mustn't show Mummy how unspeakably frightened I am. She has enough to worry about. So for God's sake shsh!"*

Similar events are recalled by others in our group, and all responded by shielding their parents from additional worry by hiding the depth of their own terror. Certainly the older members of our group, who had to face life on their own, and were thrust into early independence and responsibility, were able to cope with the challenge. Kurt sums this up for them:

> *"I often compare the lives of my children, when they were between 14 and 30 years old, with mine. While the young people of the 70s and 80s have had their own problems, we in fact benefitted from the consequences of penniless emigration. From the moment we left school we had to fend for ourselves. That was the best experience possible and something that would not have happened to me in other circumstances. This was a positive influence on my attitude to life, which is - no matter what happens I shall manage."*

CONCLUDING REFLECTIONS

This narrative sets out to explore how the attitudes of ten people have been affected by the experience of having been child refugees from the Nazi regime, growing up in wartime Britain as 'enemy aliens'. Although I did have my own hidden agenda, I wanted members of the group to set out their own priorities so that 'The Common Threads' would emerge spontaneously. And they did! It soon became apparent that all of them had been high achievers at school and college; that they all had a driving urge to succeed; that they all were committed to making a contribution, however modest, to creating a fairer and more harmonious society. The work ethic is clearly very strong in all of us. There is an unexpressed need to justify our existence. For some this is apparent in a special effort undertaken to fulfil the imagined hopes of absent parents. For others it was a direct response to our parents' encouragement and expectations. They wanted us to succeed in the new homeland which they had chosen for us.

Most people in the group chose a career through which they can help to create a more just society. Paul is an outstanding example. His life has been committed to challenging injustice, prejudice, hypocrisy, double standards, and privilege, not only in the community at large but also in the established Churches to which he has given a lifetime of service. Through his broadcasts, his writings and his ministry, he has encouraged other people to work for a fairer world. This has also been one of the objectives of creating Nansen Village; the purpose of Luke's research into patient autonomy; the mission of a psychotherapist in helping those who have lost their way; and it is the avowed aim of Oxfam.

When I asked members of the group whether they had any relatives or contacts in Germany, none of them answered directly. Instead all of them responded by talking at length about their relationship with the land of their birth. Clearly the ambivalent feelings they hold arouse very strong emotions. This is true also of their attitude to Israel, about which I deliberately avoided asking direct questions; nevertheless Israel was brought up in every conversation.

It would be interesting to find out whether these attitudes have been passed on to the children of members of our group. Have they inherited a strong work ethic? Are they as strongly committed as we are to careers or causes that aim to create a fairer society? Do they feel that they have a heightened awareness of prejudice and discrimination in the community around them?

As I come to the end of my pilgrimage I ask myself why I left this exploration of my roots so late, and find my answer in the extraordinary and unexpected response which came from some of the partners and children of my witnesses. It seems that many of the memories revealed were new to them. A few of the witnesses were themselves surprised by what they had told me, for the interviews seem to have unlocked a door behind which childhood experiences had been hidden and remained half-forgotten. Having read the verbatim transcript of their interview, it was now possible to talk in depth about these traumatic memories; to admit the pain; to dare, at last, to peal off the protective layers and reveal the true nature of the terror, the moments of despair, the hurt and the anger. In her role of psychotherapist Ruth has worked professionally with many first and second generation Holocaust-affected people. She writes:

> *I see the whole issue of this silence as rooted in the human capacity for denial. It is a protective mechanism against*

intolerable knowledge - knowledge that could strain and rupture the very structures of the personality and mind. Even under normal circumstances we live in a world full of uncertainty and potential dangers, and we have to find some way of dealing with the anxiety about continuing to exist that this generates in us. Fundamentally, denial or not-knowing is an essential survival mechanism. At all levels - at that of the individual, or of the family, or of society - we 'write out', or simply 'do not know' about things that threaten the infrastructure of our version of reality. Thus the Nazi officials were able to say with impunity and accuracy to concentration camp inmates that if they survived to tell their stories they would not be believed. Stories of such ultimate primitive terror and inhumanity are the stuff of childhood nightmares, and are too threatening to our tenuous individual and collective humanity for us to bear.

When it is someone else, some other family, another country, we can feel protected by distance. But when it is members of our own family that have been damaged, destroyed, annihilated, - that cannot be distanced - only 'not allowed in', or not known. If such terrible knowledge were 'allowed in' it would expose our vulnerable condition; how helpless we are to do anything about it, helpless even to deal with the turbulent feelings it arouses in us.

This was the issue that survivors' families were caught up in. It would not have been possible to pick up the threads of their shattered lives and start again unless thoughts about the terrible past were cut off and kept firmly out of mind. Wanting their children to be free of such burdens gave parents the conscious reason they needed to keep silent about their past. But children cannot be unaffected by their parents' experiences. Survivors' children sensed the vulnerability behind their parents' often extra strong facade and felt they had to protect them by not asking questions and 'not making trouble'. An essential feature of the 'Conspiracy of Silence' is that both sides contribute to what comes to feel like an invisible, intangible, but impenetrable barrier. There is an ever-growing literature about what has been learned from various treatment programmes with first and second generation Holocaust-affected people. Much of the subject matter is painful to read, and even the therapist is under a great deal of intangible pressure to conspire with the silence and avoid putting dreaded thoughts, ideas and 'the unknowable' into words. (21)

As if to confirm all that Ruth outlined in this article, no testimony more poignant could be imagined than a letter I received from one of this 'second generation'. I quote:

"As a result of your interview with my mother I was able to read the transcript which filled such important gaps in my own history. And then she talked in a way she has never done before of what happened to her. Now it was a feeling account, not just factual; and partly as a consequence of this release she and I have made important steps forward in our relationship. We are beginning to understand ourselves and each other.

I have discovered during the last few months just how much I was affected by being born to a woman so full of insecurity and deep-rooted fear. It is as though I was born and, looking up, instinctively knew that my mother had an enormous need for reassurance and love. I coped with it, quite unconsciously, by being so sensitive to her needs that I couldn't allow myself any. I didn't accept myself as a 'needy human being' until quite recently, and I am almost 40! Understanding my heritage is a vital part of being able to cope with the anxiety and insecurity that has been passed on to me, and it is all getting much easier.

You mention that many of your interviewees have a need to justify their existence, to prove themselves in some

102

way. I have been so aware of this as part of my mother's make up, in that she never wastes a second; always doing six things at once, always feeling guilty about being lazy. She must always be 'doing', never just 'being'. Now it is as if the interview with you has allowed her the release of deeply held emotion that affected her relationship, not only with her parents but also with her children. I will make sure that my children understand their family heritage."

Eve sums up for us all with a poignant personal perspective:

"I am very close now to my only surviving cousin in Prague, and to his children. I was once showing his son, Adam, some photos of my brother and myself when we were little, and he said, 'Oh! I would have had an Uncle Tommy then!' Because I loved my brother very much, that really wrung my heart. It made me realise that there is a knock on effect of all this sorrow. Adam would have had uncles and aunts he was never to know. The effects of the Holocaust will go on and on and on."

EPILOGUE

The Holocaust was a Universal Tragedy. It was also an intensely personal tragedy for those caught in the full blast of the storm. All of us in our small group of witnesses are conscious that we are lucky to be alive. One million children perished in the camps. In Yad Vashem there is a special memorial to the children. It is a windowless domed hall, approached along a narrow curving passage. There is no sound except for a voice reciting quietly the names of the million children who died. The recording of their names will continue to be heard, endlessly. When the millionth name has been heard the first will be repeated. The darkness intensifies; one must grip a rail as a guide to continue the pilgrimage; and when all trace of daylight has been left behind, and all seems blackness, one steps suddenly into a blaze of light. A single candle burns in the vast empty black space, its light reflected in a million mirrors. One million candles - the lights of one million children - illuminate the darkness of our world.

Holocaust Memorial in Kibbutz Hazorea. Six columns represent the six million Jews who perished. My grandparents' names are inscribed at the top of the third column.

REFERENCES

Unless otherwise stated, all contributions quoted by those interviewed are taken from verbatim transcripts of our conversations recorded on:

Ida	28 November	1993	(and Memoirs for her granddaughter Emma)
Renate	18 November	1993	
Frank	28 November	1993	
Kurt	2 December	1993	
Eva	8 December	1993	
Eve	10 January	1994	
Paul	8 November	1993	
Ruth	17 February	1994	
Luke	9 December	1993	

(1)   GERSHON, Karen   *We Came As Children*
                              London Macmillan 1989
                              Introductory Letter

(2)   WHITEMAN, Dorit Bader *The Uprooted - a Hitler Legacy*
                              New York Plenum Press 1993 cover page

(3)   GERSHON, Karen   op.cit p176

(4)   TURNER, Barry   *...and The Policeman Smiled*
                              London Bloomsbury 1990 p 4

(5)   OESTREICHER, Paul   *Aufs Kreuz gelegt*
                              Berlin Wichern-Verlag 1993
                              Ein persönliches Wort an die deutschen
                              Leser S 14

(6)   RUMBOLD, Sir Horace   quoted in TURNER, Barry op.cit. p 4

(7)   WEIZMANN, Chaim   *Trial and Error*
                              London Hamish Hamilton 1949 p 434

(8)   WEIZMANN, Chaim   Manchester Guardian 23 May 1936

(9)   BETTELHEIM, Bruno   *Recollections and Reflections*
                              London Penguin 1992 p 254

(10) TURNER, Barry   op.cit p 26

(11) OESTREICHER, Paul *The Double Cross*
           London Darton Longman and Todd 1986
           p 30

(12) MAYER, Gerda   Bernini's Cat (New and Selected Poems)
           by Gerda Mayer. Iron Press 1999.
           First published in The Knockabout Show,
           Chatto and Windus 1978

(13) WHITEMAN, Dorit Bader op.cit. p 34

(14) GERSHON, Karen   op.cit. p178

(15) CRAWSHAW, Steve *The Independent*
           Saturday 12 March 1994

(16) MACARDLE, Dorothy *Children of Europe*
           London Victor Gollancz 1949
           excerpts from p 19 to 21

(17) WHITEMAN, Dorit Bader op.cit. p 34

(18) BETTELHEIM, Bruno op.cit. excerpts from p 220 to p 223

(19) WHITEMAN, Dorit Bader op.cit. p 406

(20) WHITEMAN, Dorit Bader op.cit. p 392

(21) BARNETT, Ruth   unpublished article about the psychology of
           Holocaust-affected people

BIBLIOGRAPHY

ARCHIVES

CENTRAL BRITISH FUND for WORLD JEWISH RELIEF
Unpublished records held at Drayton House, London

GENERAL TEXTS

ANDREWS, Molly — *Lifetimes of Commitment*
Cambridge   CUP   1991

BEAGLEHOLE, Ann — *A Small Price to Pay - Refugees from Hitler in New Zealand 1939 - 1946*
Wellington   NZ   Allen and Unwin   1988

BENTWICH, Norman — *They Found Refuge*
London   Cresset Press   1956

BETTELHEIM, Bruno — *Recollections and Reflections*
London   Penguin   1992

DARTON, Lawrence — *Friends Committee for Jews and Aliens 1933 - 1950*
Society of Friends   1952

EPSTEIN, Helen — *Children of the Holocaust*
New York   Bantum Books   1981

GERSHON, Karen — *We Came as Children*
London   Macmillan   1989

HUSSAR, Bruno — *When the cloud lifted - The Testimony of an Israeli Priest*
Dublin   Veritas   1989

NOREN HANF, Catherine — *The Camera of My Family*
New York   Alfred A Knopf   1976

OESTREICHER, Paul — *The Double Cross*
London   Darton Longman and Todd   1986

OESTREICHER, Paul — *Aufs Kreuz gelegt*
Berlin   Wichern-Verlag   1993

SHERMAN, A. J. — *Island Refuge: Britain and the Refugees from the Third Reich 1933 - 1939*
London   Paul Elek   1973

SILMAN-CHEONG, Helen — *Wellesley Aron Rebel With a Cause*
London   Valentine Mitchell   1992

TURNER, Barry — *...and the Policeman Smiled*
London   Bloomsbury   1991

WEIZMANN, Chaim — *Trial and Error*
London   Hamish Hamilton   1949

WHITEMAN, Dorit Bader — *The Uprooted - A Hitler Legacy*
New York   Plenum Press   1993